Life Journey and the Old Testament

Life Journey and the Old Testament

An Experiential Approach to the Bible and Personal Transformation

Conrad E. L'Heureux

FOREWORD BY JOHN A. SANFORD

PAULIST PRESS
New York/Mahwah

Library of Congress Cataloging-in-Publication Data

L'Heureux, Conrad E.
      Life journey and the Old Testament.

      Includes bibliographies.
      1. Bible.   O.T.—Criticism, interpretation, etc.
2. Regeneration (Theology)   3. Spiritual life.
4. L'Heureux, Conrad E.   I. Title.
BS1171.2.L56   1986   220.6   86-9339
ISBN 0-8091-2828-4 (pbk.)

Published by Paulist Press
997 Macarthur Boulevard
Mahwah, New Jersey 07430

Printed and bound in the
United States of America

Contents

This book is dedicated to my aunt
Eva M. Tondreau
whose love and encouragement
I have always been able to count on.

John A. Sanford

Foreword

I well remember that when I was a theological student my most helpful courses were in biblical studies. My professors of the Old and New Testaments, steeped as they were in historical criticism, had a great deal to teach me, and what they had to say opened my eyes to the history, origin, and literature of the Bible. However, when I was compelled by life to work out my personal problems what I learned in seminary about the Bible did not help me. Perhaps, I wondered, the Bible isn't supposed to help us in our personal life? But that possibility was not satisfactory to me, for of what value was a religious faith if it could not help you understand and face what was happening in your life? Later, as I was able to relate to the process of healing that was taking place within me, the personal meaning of many of the biblical narratives became clear to me. They then deepened my knowledge of myself and helped me on my personal life journey.

If when I was a seminary student I had taken Bible classes from Conrad L'Heureux or been able to read his book LIFE JOURNEY AND THE OLD TESTAMENT, I would have been helped by the Bible much earlier in my life. For L'Heureux and his book do what my biblical professors had not attempted to do in their classes: relate biblical stories and themes to personal life without sacrificing the valuable perspective of historical criticism.

It is a pleasure to read this book because it is so well-written. L'Heureux is able to express himself in a clear and lively fashion. He does not feel it is beneath him to descend to the level of the lay person in order to inform him or her in a clear way of the contributions of historical criticism to our knowledge of the Bible. But at the same time he demonstrates the rare gift of being able to do this without losing the depth of his message.

Professor L'Heureux tells us in the introduction how he happened to write the book. He is a professor of the Old Testament, but at a certain point in his life he felt the need, as I did at one time, to relate his biblical knowledge to his inner development. He tells us that he sensed that many biblical stories intersected with his own experience but his purely academic approach to the Bible did not clarify for him how this was so. L'Heureux then immersed himself in self-exploration and programs aiming at psychological and spiritual growth. As he did so it became clear to him that the important themes of the Bible were indeed his own personally important themes. The personal perspective from which L'Heureux writes makes his book alive to the reader, but at the same time he is never an obtrusive author. Although he tells us of his experiences he focuses our attention not on himself but on his students, on ourselves, and on the general experiences of all people who are seeking for help in their lives.

L'Heureux selected four excellent sections from the Bible for presentation and discussion: the story of King David; the calls extended by God to persons such as Moses, Gideon, and Isaiah; the theme of faith and trust; motifs of healing in the psalms. For each section he first presents the insights of historical criticism, and then follows with examples of how he taught the personal side of the stories to his students through unique classroom experiential methods. These methods included the use of imagery, introspection, group discussion, and a Socratic method of interaction between himself and the members of the class. These must have been lively classes indeed, and L'Heureux brings them back to life for us in this book. He presents them, however, not as rules of "this is how it is to be done," but as guidelines for our own creative process and thinking.

The author says that his book is written to colleagues, to those who are seeking for meaning in their lives, to those in the human potential movement, and to those in the field of religious education. Certainly the book will be of value to persons in all of these categories, but it will be of special value to those involved in religious education. Whether the teacher is a professor in a seminary or a lay person teaching in CCD, this book will impart sound information and new ideas. In addition, there is an appendix which summarizes in a succinct and brilliant way the history and essence of the historical criticism of the Bible, and this should be especially helpful to the lay religious educator.

Only one thing is missing in the book. L'Heureux gives the religious educator many examples of and guidelines for creative ways of teaching biblical material. He does not point out, however, that these methods will only work if the teacher himself or herself has undergone a creative inner process. A non-creative person cannot teach creatively even with the best of guidance. L'Heureux is himself an example of a teacher who, through his own process of daring and creative self-exploration, unlocked the door to creative teaching. One cannot mimic him and become the creative teacher, but one can follow his example and become a more creative person, and then use his methods, or new ones emerging from within oneself, and creative teaching will be the result. This point, however, should not dissuade the reader from using L'Heureux's methods; it should only spur the reader on toward his or her personal growth.

Introduction

O ur culture, in the last part of the twentieth century, seems far removed from Old Testament times. It is not surprising that many people today wonder whether it is still possible to approach the Old Testament in a way which fosters personal and spiritual growth. *Life Journey and the Old Testament* not only answers this question affirmatively, it also presents a unique perspective which allows us to establish fresh connections with the Bible's power to transform human lives. Though the primary focus is on the Old Testament, the core of what this book has to say applies to the New Testament as well.

The methodology known as historical criticism reigns supreme in modern academic study of the Bible. This historico-critical approach will be described in detail in the Appendix where both its positive contributions and its limits are defined. For the time being, let it suffice to say that the historico-critical method in research and teaching has attempted to study the Bible in a "scientific and objective" manner. The scholars who have accepted this method, including myself, did so in the hope that the detached and historical point of view displayed by the critical method was in fact the approach which would make it possible for us to really understand what the Bible was about.

During the first ten years of my career as a university professor in Old Testament, my research and teaching concentrated almost exclusively on the historico-critical method and the conclusions to which it leads. Eventually, however, I began to listen more seriously to both colleagues and students who were talking about the limitations of the critical approach. What they were saying, essentially, is that no matter how insightful and interesting the scholarship was, it did not relate in a significant way to people's lives. No matter how hard we tried to make the ideas practical and relevant, there was something crucial that was missing. And no matter how much further we pushed along in the direction of historical criticism, we were not getting any closer to that "missing something."

Struggling to find ways of bridging the gap between scholarship and the existential concerns of human persons, I asked myself what it was about the Old Testament that was significant for me in a personal way. Certain passages came to mind, and I realized that their significance for me was not always determined by academic considerations. It was more important that certain stories in the Bible intersected with my experience in a way which seemed to illuminate my life, providing me support and guidance. I can best elaborate what I mean by giving a few examples of such passages.

First, there is the story of Abraham, who left behind his homeland, his family, and the gods he had hitherto worshipped, in order to follow the call of a God he had not known before. The patriarch set out on a journey to a land he knew nothing about except that it had been promised to him by the God who called him. In my own life, I have sometimes felt that I was making a new beginning which required that I leave behind much of my past. Sometimes I saw these new beginnings as a response to a call from God, while at other times they seemed to be simple practical decisions which I had reached after weighing the pros and cons. Either way, in many of these situations, I had little understanding of what would lie ahead for me. I learned from the story of Abraham that I needed to trust that by answering the call, I was moving in a direction of growth, journeying towards what was for me the land of promise. I derived support and encouragement by looking at the model provided by Abraham in his journey. By looking at that model, I was able to move on, in spite of uncertainty and fear.

A second example comes from the series of stories about the Exodus from Egypt and the subsequent wandering in the wilderness. The Israelites had undergone a long period of oppressive slavery under the pharaohs. Their journey out of slavery into freedom under the leadership of Moses is depicted in the Old Testament as the greatest and most important saving intervention of God on their behalf. However, in the stories about the travelling of the people through the desert, there is an interesting phenomenon: time after time, the escaped slaves became discouraged at the difficulty of being responsible for themselves and entertained the possibility of returning to the comfort and security of slavery! Of course, I have never been a slave in the social or political sense. But I have experienced many forms of psychological or spiritual slavery. For example, when my fear of rejection kept me from making overtures to other persons; when my need to gain recognition from others drove me to work compulsively; when my addiction to food or alcohol threatened my physical health; or when a misguided sense of guilt led me into self-destructive patterns of behavior. If the central saving activity of God in the Old Testament is to call and to lead persons out of slavery, then I can see my own response to the call to growth as a process in continuity with the biblical tradition. I can experience myself as a participant in the Exodus, part of something larger than my individual life, an element in a larger picture of meaning. Furthermore, like the Israelites, I sometimes feel that the responsibility of freedom gets rather demanding and a return to Egypt begins to look attractive. But the story of their journey from slavery to freedom helps give meaning and significance to my own struggle. It reminds me of the direction in which I have to journey in order to continue growing and learning.

Yet another passage which has long been important to me is part of the story of King David. I am referring specifically to a series of episodes contained in 2 Sam 15–19. David's son Absalom has started a political uprising against his father which has forced the old king to abandon his capital, Jerusalem, and to journey into exile. In spite of the enormity of Absalom's offense, David instructs the soldiers fighting for him not to injure the rebellious son. When in fact Absalom is killed in battle, David is so overcome with grief that he keeps crying, "O my son Absalom, O my son, my son Absalom. I wish I had died instead of you (2 Sam 19:1)." David's warning to the soldiers as well as the bitterness of his mourning testifies to the intensity of a father's love for his son, a love whose power I have always found deeply moving. At the same time, the passage raises questions: "Did the emotional attachment of David as father blind him to the destructiveness of his child and cause David the king to neglect the best interests of the people he ruled? Can a father's love go too far?" I remember how insistent these questions were to me when I was teaching this material during the months my wife and I were expecting our first child. David so epitomized the depth of human feeling, the nature of love and parenthood, that I wanted to name our first child after him if it was a boy. So one of the journeys taken by the great king of Israel intersected with my own life journey at a particular point where a connection was established. My effort to understand David was identical with my struggle to understand the meaning of love and parenthood.

In the preceding examples, my own life journey connected with the journeys of either the whole Israelite community or individual members of that community. I began to see that these connections provide the key to making the Bible significant and relevant in our lives. My conviction was reinforced by reading some of the works of John Sanford, an Episcopalian priest and Jungian psychoanalyst. In *The Man Who Wrestled with God* (Ramsey, NJ: Paulist Press, 1981) and *King Saul, a Tragic Hero* (Ramsey, NJ: Paulist Press, 1985) Sanford shows concretely how Old Testament stories can be taken as archetypal formulations of "the most important and fundamental process which goes on in human life: the transformation of human beings from ego-centric, unconscious persons, to persons of wholeness, breadth of vision, and spiritual awareness (*The Man Who Wrestled with God*, p. 5)." This process, called individuation in the psychology of Carl Jung, is embodied in ancient stories about the transformative journey. The same process unfolds in each of our individual lives as we journey towards growth and wholeness. The Jungian perspective, as explicated by Sanford, provides a helpful theoretical background for understanding the relationship between the biblical stories and our own lives.

The key, then, to making the Old Testament significant for us today lies in establishing connections between the stories of ancient Israel and our own personal stories. But the question still remains, "How can I study and teach the Old Testament in such a way that these connections can be made?" My own answer to this question came to me in a somewhat roundabout manner.

Several years ago, just about the time I reached the age of forty, I became interested in self-exploration and psychological growth. This was quite a new departure for me. Until then, I was very much afraid of what I would find if I started examining who I was. Because of this fear, I had, in the past, rather contemptuously dismissed activities which sought to promote self-knowledge and growth. Finally, through a combination of circumstances, I joined with my wife in attending a workshop on communication and relationships. The workshop was so enjoyable and proved so helpful to me that I sought out more experiences of the same type. Over the next few years I attended a large number of seminars, workshops and retreats on topics such as self-esteem, unconditional love, interpretation of dreams, brain research, healing, holistic spirituality and Gestalt Therapy. I investigated a type of literature which was new to me and I was especially influenced by the writings of John Powell, Matthew Fox, Carl Jung, Ken Keyes, Barry Neil Kaufman, Jean Houston, Joseph Campbell, Gerald Jampolski and John Sanford. Also, by attending conferences of the Association for Humanistic Psychology, I gained experience in the techniques characteristic of the "human potential movement." I also took graduate courses in the Department of Counseling at my university and even explored yoga and Zen Buddhism.

Involvement in all these activities had concrete results in my life. I became much more comfortable with the world of feelings and learned to relate with other persons on a level which is much more open, trusting and loving. Instead of striving desperately to receive acknowledgement from other people, I began to find more satisfaction from within, just being true to who I am. My old predominantly rational approach to life was balanced by making room for feeling and intuition. Letting go of the skepticism which a more rationalistic perspective had urged upon me for a period, I found a renewed trust in my own spiritual experience. Meditation and prayer became a more regular part of my life. Physical exercise, too, was now part of my routine. As a result of a change of diet I lost over fifty pounds and felt healthier than I had ever felt before. I not only looked better, but my life was fuller, richer and more satisfying.

With all the positive developments deriving from my new involvements, I began to wonder how I might help other people share these benefits. It is surprising that I did not see the connection at first and that it came to me as a kind of sudden insight. What I began to realize is that much of the new learning I delighted in was there all the time in the Old Testament. This applies in two ways. First, much of the conceptual content of my new discoveries was actually found in the Bible. Secondly, many of the techniques used in group process were admirably suited for use with biblical material. So to share my new learning with others all I had to do was continue what I was already doing: teaching the Old Testament. Except that I would have to go about it in a different way. I began to experiment in my university classes and in adult education classes which I taught in local parishes. I used experiential group process as a way of relating to the Old Testament. Not all the experiments were successful, but as I took more risks in trying new ideas, I became more convinced that this was a powerful and effective way of letting the transformative power of the Bible touch people in a way which helped them along in their life journeys. *Life Journey and the Old Testament* is a description of the more successful of these experiments.

The four chapters of *Life Journey and the Old Testament* present detailed reports on the use of experiential group process with four different blocks of Old Testament material. The first chapter, on the Davidic Court History, uses a single lengthy narrative. In my second chapter, I focus on a number of shorter narratives, each dealing with the same theme, that of the call. Next, the theological ideas connected with a single Hebrew key-word provide the starting point for work on the relationship between trust and fear. Finally, the Lament of the Individual, a specific form-critical category from the Psalms, is examined from the point of view of sickness and healing. These four chapters constitute four separate examples of the method I am exploring. Each of the chapters is independent, so they may be read in any sequence. Taken as a whole, they illustrate the great variety which is available in selecting biblical starting points for experiential group process.

My intention is not to reject and by-pass the insights gained from academic study of the Bible, but to integrate the contributions of historical criticism and then move beyond its limitations. Consequently, each chapter includes discussion of the results of critical investigation. A rather thorough review of research is presented in the first chapter. This will give the reader who is not trained in biblical studies a concrete picture of the kinds of questions which occupy scholars. In chapters 2 to 4, the survey of scholarship is limited to matters which bear more directly on the experiential exercises described in the chapter. The precise nature of the relationship between the critical study and the more subjective personal appropriation is a matter I have not tried to define beforehand but which I believe must emerge from a posteriori reflection based on a much larger body of data. This issue will require further discussion at a later time.

The decision to present the four chapters in the format of reports on my experience as a teacher and group leader was a deliberate one. At one point, I considered the possibility of employing something of a "how to" format which would guide others in imitating what I have done. There were two reasons for rejecting that idea. First, I still consider my work to be at an experimental stage and want to avoid giving the impression that this is *the way* to do it. Secondly, and much more importantly, there are no simple shortcuts to the personal appropriation of the biblical stories. It is important for other teachers and group leaders to trust their own convictions about what is personally significant in the Bible. They need to be doing their own inner work on the issues which are important for them if they hope to facilitate the work done by others. Finally, the style of working with a group will vary tremendously, depending upon the personality of the individual. Consequently, my hope is that others will take what I present in this book as an example of what one person has done and then use their own creativity in moving towards what works for them. At the same time, I believe that much of what I describe can indeed be adapted for use by other group leaders. I will be eager to hear reports about how this has worked out for them.

The principal audience I have had in mind while writing this book consists of persons in the field of religious education. They are the ones who, more than anyone else, have struggled with the problem of what to do with their academic training in Bible once they entered a practical teaching situation. I hope that the direction I am pointing to will help them to become more effective in their work. The same applies to related forms of ministry such as retreat work, youth ministry, and others. How far college and university teachers will want to go in adapting these techniques remains to be seen. While I recognize the legitimacy of the distinction between university education and the ministry of the church, I believe that the former is far too exclusively oriented to purely intellectual matters. A more wholistic philosophy of education would allow the incorporation of much of what I propose in this book without compromise of academic integrity. This is clearly an issue which will require further discussion.

Life Journey and the Old Testament is also addressed to my colleagues in biblical studies and in theology, especially those working in the area of hermeneutics. There is a basic paradigm which underlies much of the current discussion of this topic. The pattern which seems to be taken for granted, both by specialists and by students, begins with the historico-critical exegesis of individual passages. It is assumed that the study of individual passages would lead to a more generalizing kind of summary or overview, i.e. Old Testament theology, which would still be principally on the descriptive level. Finally, there would come the "practical application" in the life of the individual student or those to whom that person intends to minister. It has become increasingly clear to me that the preceding paradigm is overly rationalistic. To leave the "personal application" as a final step, for which the instructor often abdicates any responsibility, means that it is virtually impossible for this application ever to take place. The method described in *Life Journey and the Old Testament* suggests that the movement back and forth between personal and descriptive considerations is vastly more intricate. In order for study of the Bible to have significant impact on people's lives, the legitimate presence of the personal element needs to be admitted from the very start. Consequently, the contribution of this book is likely to greatly complicate the theoretical discussion of hermeneutics and of the relationships among exegesis, biblical theology and personal appropriation. On the other hand, the discussion found in the Appendix will more clearly define the boundary between the positive contribution and the limitations of historical criticism. As such, it may help to defuse some of the antagonism between the scholars who have emerged as critics of the historico-critical method and those who, sensing themselves under attack, have felt the need to defend the integrity of the scholarly enterprise.

Yet another segment of readers who will find *Life Journey and the Old Testament* helpful consists of individuals who are seeking to discover how the Old Testament can enrich their personal lives, furthering them along in their own life journeys. With these readers in mind, I have tried to present each chapter in such a way that no previous knowledge of biblical scholarship is presumed. My intention is that the book be available to the largest possible readership, even though this means that professional colleagues will find much they can skim over because it is already well known to them.

I also believe that persons connected with the human potential movement, or interested in wholistic approaches to health and education, will benefit from this book. I have learned much from them. I want my contribution to help them see a little more clearly that many of their concerns are in profound harmony with the ancient literary heritage of the Western religious tradition.

Finally, I want to say that *Life Journey and the Old Testament,* more than anything else I have written, is a reflection of my own life journey. It grows out of the path I have travelled so far and manifests who I am as a person at this stage of my journey. I hope that it will touch other travellers in a way which empowers them to be true to their own calling, to honor and value their own path, and to become all that they can be.

Chapter One

David's Story and Our Story

The stories about King David preserved in the Old Testament are superb examples of the story-teller's art, containing the power to move us profoundly as they explore the whole range and depth of human emotion. In the terminology of psychologist Carl Jung, we can say that they are full of archetypal symbols. The specific narrative which we will be dealing with is contained in the Second Book of Samuel, chapters 9 through 20 and the First Book of Kings, chapters 1 and 2. In the modern discussion of this material, it is usually referred to as the Davidic Court History or the Succession Narrative. We will begin with a summary of the story. This will be followed by an overview which gives the reader an idea of what kinds of issues are discussed in the historico-critical study of these chapters. Finally, I will report on a group process approach to the use of the material. Naturally, it is better to read the actual biblical account rather than my brief summary, and those readers who choose to go to the original could skip the section which follows.

1. The Davidic Court History: A Summary

To some extent the story starts in the middle of things. There are some matters which would have been very familiar to the ancient reader of the story but which might not be known to everyone today. Among these is the fact that David was the successor to King Saul, the very first king Israel ever had. Before Saul, the twelve tribes had been organized as a tribal federation which had provided a great deal of freedom for the individual tribes. In those days the most noteworthy figures were military leaders called "judges." The rise of the monarchy had been made necessary because neighboring peoples posed a military threat which the loosely knit tribal structure could not resist effectively. So Saul, a man from the tribe of Benjamin, had been appointed king, but not without strong reservations from the traditionalists who feared that the monarchy would become an oppressive institution. Even during Saul's lifetime, a young warrior named David, from the tribe of Judah, acquired a degree of fame and reputation which Saul perceived as a challenge. Although David was married to Saul's daughter Michal and had Saul's son Jonathan as an intimate friend, the old king sought to kill his young rival. Eventually, Saul and Jonathan both died in a battle against the Philistines, and David was recognized as king by the people of the tribe of Judah and anointed at Hebron. Meanwhile, the northern tribes recognized Saul's son Ishbosheth (or Ishbaal) as legitimate successor to the throne. Through a complicated series of events, involving intrigue and betrayal, most members of Saul's family, including Ishbosheth, were killed. Then the northern tribes joined Judah in recognizing David. Eventually, he moved his capital to Jerusalem, a city which had remained under Jebusite, or Canaanite, control until captured by David and his men.

The Court History proper opens in 2 Sam 9 with David's inquiry as to whether there remain any living survivors from Saul's family. He is informed that there is a handicapped young man named Mephibosheth, or Meribbaal,[1] grandson of Saul and son of Jonathan, who had been David's closest friend.

David summons Mephibosheth to Jerusalem where he will have the privilege of living at the court and eating at the king's table. The estate which had belonged to Saul is restored to Mephibosheth and will be managed by the latter's servant Ziba. These acts are presented as deriving from David's kindness and loyalty, but his self-interest is also involved: Mephibosheth, as sole surviving descendant of Saul, was potentially a rival claimant to the throne and David now had him where he could keep an eye on him.

Moving on to chapter 10, we learn how David went to war with the Ammonites. One might get the impression that this has nothing to do with what went before. As the story progresses, however, each of these episodes will fall into place as part of a tightly woven plot. What we are told here is that David had magnanimously sent representatives to offer condolences to the new heir to the Ammonite throne upon the death of the latter's father. But the advisors of the Ammonite King suggest that David's emissaries are really spying out the city to discover how David could conquer it. The messengers sent by David are therefore humiliated and sent back in disgrace. War breaks out over this event and as a result David not only takes over the Ammonite kingdom, but also defeats the Arameans (or Syrians) who had allied themselves to Ammon in the fight against David.

We are getting a little ahead of events, however. For the fateful episode of our drama takes place while David's army, led by his commander Joab, was besieging the Ammonite capital of Rabbah. King David had stayed behind in Jerusalem. From the vantage point of the palace roof he observed a beautiful woman bathing in the courtyard of her house. It was Bathsheba, wife of Uriah the Hittite, one of David's soldiers who was at that very moment out at war. David summoned Bathsheba, slept with her, and later found out she was pregnant. In an attempt to cover up the adultery, he finds a pretext to have Uriah return from the front, hoping he will sleep with Bathsheba and not figure out later on that someone else had made her pregnant. When Uriah does not go home to his wife, David plots his death by ordering Joab to put him in a fighting position where he is sure to get killed. Then Bathsheba joins David and gives birth to his child.

At this point (chapter 12) the prophet Nathan enters the scene. He tells David a story about a rich man who owned many flocks and herds but nonetheless took and killed the one little ewe lamb which was the only possession of a poor man who lived in the same city. Outraged at the injustice, the king declares that the guilty man deserves to die. Nathan retorts, "You are the man." The king's sins of lust and violence will come back to plague him. Because David admits the crime, it is forgiven and his life is spared. However, the child born of the unlawful union will die. The baby's death is dramatically recounted. Afterwards, Bathsheba bears another son, Solomon, about whom we are told, "The Lord loved him."

Now a plot begins to unfold in which we see the flaws in David's character being mirrored in the actions of his own children. We find a chain of tragic events in which his downfall seems as ineluctable as the nemesis which engulfs the characters in Greek tragedy. His oldest son Amnon, heir apparent to the throne, is also heir to David's lust. He contrives for the opportunity to be alone with his half-sister Tamar with whom he is desperately in love. He rapes her then scornfully sends her away in disgrace. King David is angry at this, but fails to carry out his responsibility to execute justice. However, Tamar's full brother Absalom nurses his anger for Amnon, waiting for a chance to strike. When the opportunity presents itself, he shows himself equal in violence to his father by killing his brother Amnon after getting him drunk. Absalom then flees the country, to escape punishment from David. Once again the king does nothing. Eventually, father and son are reconciled and Absalom returns to Jerusalem.

With Amnon out of the way, Absalom is next in line for the throne. He can not wait, however. While his father is still alive, he gains the support of disaffected subjects, gathers a coterie of supporters and goes to Hebron where he is acclaimed as king. Then, in full rebellion, he marches against his father and Jerusalem. David, meanwhile, has heard of the uprising and decided to abandon his capital city. The priests suggest that the ark of the covenant be taken along. David appears to believe that such an action would amount to manipulation of God. He tells the priests to remain in Jerusalem with the ark, trusting that if it is indeed God's will, He will bring him back. David and his entourage descend to the Kidron Valley and up the Mount of Olives, in full mourning, more like a procession of penitents than the march of a glorious king. News is brought that the wise counsellor Ahithophel has joined the rebels. David's response is to utter a simple prayer, "O Yahweh, change Ahithophel's counsel into foolishness (2 Sam 15:31)." The very next verse informs us that as David reaches a holy place on the summit of the Mount of Olives, he meets the faithful Hushai. Though David does not yet realize it, this is the answer to his prayer. Finally, the company is accosted by a Benjaminite named Shimei who curses David, accusing him of being responsible for the massacre of the family of Saul (another Benjaminite). David's henchmen want to cut Shimei down, but David once again prefers to leave matters in Yahweh's hands.

Meanwhile, back in Jerusalem, Absalom is trying to make a policy decision. The counsellor Ahithophel suggests a lightning strike which will catch David and his men unawares, and bring the change of regime to a definitive conclusion. Hushai, pretending to be among the conspirators though he is secretly on David's side, presents a different view. He argues that it would be better for Absalom to wait until he can assemble a full army before he attempts to contend with such trained tacticians as David and his men. Absalom is convinced by Hushai's argument, and although all of this unfolds in a manner which is completely natural, the narrator informs us that the reason Absalom made this choice was that "Yahweh had decided to defeat the good counsel of Ahithophel so that He might bring about the downfall of Absalom (2 Sam 17:14)." In other words, when the king had humbly placed his fate in the hands of God and prayed for help, the prayer was answered.

The delay provided by the fact that Absalom followed Hushai's advice gave David time to organize his forces before the battle actually took place. The most interesting detail in the report of this engagement, found in chapter 18, is that David's main concern seems to be for Absalom. He gave orders that the rebellious son, who had led the country into full scale civil war, was not to be harmed! But his wishes were not respected. Absalom's hair got caught in a tree as he was fleeing on his mule. While he hung there, Joab had him killed. There is irony in this as the narrative had previously informed us that Absalom had the custom of having his hair publicly cut and weighed each year to show off his manliness. The basis of his vanity then became the means of his downfall. As to why Joab went directly against the wishes of David, we can only guess.

When the news of Absalom's death was brought to David, he was overcome with grief. He kept crying, "O my son Absalom. O Absalom, my son, my son. I wish I had died instead of you." The depth of the father's love is moving. Yet it seems to go to a bizarre extreme, totally beyond control. When Joab criticizes David for caring more about the rebel leader than about the loyal troops who saved his kingdom for him at the risk of their lives, David acknowledges his excess.

Anyhow, David has emerged victorious and the march

back to Jerusalem is about to begin. To win over the surviving partisans of the revolt, David appoints Amasa, the commander of Absalom's forces, over his own army in the place of Joab. Shimei, who had cursed David, begs for pardon and David promises never to harm him. A squabble over whether Mephibosheth had intended to join Absalom's rebellion in the hopes of restoring the house of Saul with himself as ruler can not be settled and ends in compromise. A powerful elder who had supplied David with provisions during his exile is promised a reward. All is not well in the kingdom, however, for David's return is clouded by ongoing rivalry between Judah and the northern tribes.

The lack of unity in David's kingdom erupts one more time in a revolt led by Sheba (a Benjaminite again!) and reported in chapter 20. Amasa, David's new army commander, is slow in organizing the military forces. So Joab takes matters into his own hands. By stealth he kills Amasa and takes back control of the military. The rebel leader has taken refuge in a northern city. Joab pursues him and arranges to have him killed, thus quelling the revolt.

Our tale continues in chapter 1 of 1 Kings. David is old and sick. The most beautiful young virgin in the country is sought out. When she is found, she is brought to David to be his nurse and to sleep with him if he so wishes. We are told that he did not have intercourse with her. His virility had flagged to the point where it could not be revived! This failure is linked to what follows. Adonijah, next in line for the throne according to the precedence of age, is acclaimed king with the support of Joab and a priest named Abiathar. When Nathan hears of it he acts quickly and decisively. He tells Bathsheba to say to David that he had promised that it would be *her* son, Solomon, who would reign in his place. Prodded by Nathan and Bathsheba, we are told, David instructed the other high priest, Zadok, accompanied by a military leader named Benaiah, to anoint Solomon as king. Adonijah claims sanctuary and receives a pardon while his party flees in panic.

Finally, in 1 Kgs 2, the reader is informed that on his deathbed, David summoned Solomon to give him final instructions. Solomon was to be faithful to God's law and act favorably towards persons who had been David's benefactors. However, certain villainous individuals had to get what was coming to them. Joab had brought bloodguilt upon David by killing two innocent men: Amasa and Abner (the latter in an episode not actually included in the Court History). He was not to be allowed to die peacefully in old age! The same applied to Shimei, who had cursed David. Though the father had promised not to harm the man, this promise did not apply to the son who should do what was "right." Having left this grizzly testament, David died.

In the final verses of our narrative, we learn that Solomon actually gave a reprieve to his father's enemies. However, Adonijah made a mistake which Solomon used as reason to have him executed. Joab was a victim of the same purge. The high priest Abiathar got by with merely being exiled. As to Shimei, he did not observe the conditions laid down by Solomon, and that justified his execution too. All possible threats have been disposed of and, as the narrative concludes, "The kingdom was firmly in the power of Solomon."

2. Historico-Critical Issues

In recent years, extensive scholarly work has been done on the Davidic Court History. Not all of it can be reviewed in detail. Nonetheless, this section will provide the reader with an overview of the kinds of problems which are dealt with in the historico-critical analysis of the narrative we have just summarized.

First we need to make just a few points about the approach taken to this section of the Bible. It is universally recognized that the division into "books" which we have in our modern Bibles is artificial. The main reason why the material is divided into sections which we label "Second Samuel, First Kings," etc., is that those "books" were about as much text as could comfortably be included on one leather scroll. These scrolls became very awkward to handle if they were too large. So the books of Samuel and Kings are not independent entities, but parts of a larger whole. Almost everybody today agrees that the larger whole in question originally included most of what is now in the book of Deuteronomy, along with Joshua, Judges, 1–2 Samuel, 1–2 Kings. Scholars call this large block of text the Deuteronomic History. The final editing of the great historical survey took place during the Babylonian exile in the 6th century B.C. Viewing these books as a literary whole, however, does not mean to affirm that they are a *literary unity*. For the persons who produced the Deuteronomic History were essentially *compilers* who brought together literary material from a great variety of pre-existing sources and edited it into the larger whole. Among the sources used were a collection of legal texts, annalistic reports about the kings preserved in official archives, popular legends about the prophets, and many others. This brings us to the Court History.

The generally accepted view among historico-critical scholars is that the Court History is one of the pre-existing literary units which was incorporated into the Deuteronomic History. The internal unity of the Court History was argued in a work published in German in 1926 by L. Rost.[2] His view was that when one examines the way in which the individual episodes in the story are linked together, it becomes apparent that nothing can be taken out without creating a gap in the plot. Such a tightly knit structure must, at least in the essentials, be a unified composition by a single author, as is supported by the consistency of literary style throughout the work. Moreover, the incorporation of the Court History into the larger Deuteronomic History left the original largely intact. Of course, there was the insertion of the materials which we now label 2 Sam 21–24 which the editor had to slip in before the account of David's death. Also, there were some Deuteronomic touches at the beginning of 1 Kings 2. Essentially, however, the Deuteronomic compiler(s) incorporated the Court History without tampering with it. These conclusions of Rost's were very widely accepted among scholars for several decades.

Closely related to the question of the unity of a passage is the matter of establishing its limits, that is, where does this pericope begin and where does it end. As to the ending of the Court History, there is such a clearcut conclusion at the end of 1 Kings 2, that little room remains for debate. There is a problem about the beginning, however, since 2 Sam 9 starts so abruptly right in the middle of things. In his standard-setting study of 1926, Rost had suggested that some of the material which is now in chapters 6 and 7 of 2 Samuel had, in somewhat different form, originally constituted the beginning of the Court History. Some later scholars followed his lead in this regard, though there was not as much unanimity on this issue as there was on the question of the unity of the Court History.

On this issue of unity, the consensus was so strongly in favor of Rost's position that a scholar who, in 1981, published an article questioning the unity of the Court History, felt he was in a position of going against what had almost become a critical orthodoxy.[3] However, even before that article was published, there was a growing number of dissenting voices. The situation today is that the majority still sides with Rost although there are a number of serious and important studies which view the Court History as the end product of a more complicated compositional history. To take just one example, we can turn to the recent "Anchor Bible" commentary on 2 Samuel, written by P. Kyle McCarter. McCarter relies heavily on the fact that 1 Kings 1–2 appears to be very heavily dominated by the effort to legitimate Solomon's claim to the throne and to exculpate Solomon from any blame in connection with the acts of violence which took place early in his reign (killing of Adonijah, Joab, and Shimei; exile of the high priest Abiathar). This much at least was surely written by an author who sided with Solomon and would have written early in that king's reign in order to support his regime. McCarter calls this kind of literature "court apologetic." Other authors more bluntly call it royal propaganda. The pro-Solomonic author, according to McCarter, made use of pre-existing written materials which, in turn, had been documents of "court apologetic" in favor of David. The longest of these was the account of the Absalom revolt (2 Sam 13–20) which was originally intended to justify David's behavior in that conflict. The other original unit, now divided into scattered parts (2 Sam 21:1–14 and 9:1–13), was an account of David's dealings with the family of Saul, exonerating David of any culpability in their virtual extinction. McCarter's view of the origins of the Court History, then, is that originally pro-David stories were given a new context to serve pro-Solomon purposes by the addition of the last two chapters, and other editorial modifications.

It will be seen that the understanding of the compositional and editorial history of the Court History by McCarter is closely linked to the question of political bias. This issue was already raised in Rost's 1926 study and has more recently been the object of intense study.[4] Several authors have independently argued that in fact the narrative of the Court History was originally *anti*-monarchical and that it is only a later editorial reworking of the text which gave it a pro-Davidic and/or pro-

Solomonic slant. These theories are summarized by Mc-
Carter, who also includes a full bibliography.

Another area of discussion in the scholarly literature concerns the historicity of the Court History. In an influential article entitled "The Beginnings of Historical Writing in Ancient
Israel," G. von Rad claimed that the Court History, written
during the reign of Solomon, was the first example in the
whole cultural history of the world, of the writing of genuine
history.[5] Its author, then, deserved the credit which is often
given to the Greeks Herodotus and Thucydides for this
achievement. von Rad's view that the Court History gives an
eye witness account which is factually reliable became the
dominant position in the literature. Recently, this view has
been subject to devastating criticism. R. N. Whybray, for in-
stance, argued that all the intimate personal details and the
interest in the psychological make-up of the characters could
be explained just as well if the work were fictional.[6] Rather
than label the work as "history," Whybray argues that it is
closer to a novel. Naturally, the whole thrust towards seeing
the work as propagandistic further erodes confidence in its factual reliability. One of the most recent studies, by John Van
Seters, concludes that the various episodes in the story "may
all be contrived."[7]

Another major focus of interest in recent scholarship on
the Court History has been the analysis of its quality as literature. Indeed scholarly discussion has for many decades been
full of accolades to the author of this material for the high degree of literary sophistication and power. This favorable dis-
position is now backed up by careful analyses which give more
concrete insight into the literary structure.[8]

Finally, we may ask, what of the religious message of the
work? A significant contribution to this aspect of investigation
was made by G. von Rad in the article mentioned previously.
von Rad examines the manner in which God's involvement in

historical events is represented in the Court History compared to the understanding found in older Israelite narratives such as the "hero sagas" found in the book of Judges. In the latter case, we find that God's activity is presented as being manifest in marvellous events which go beyond ordinary human experience. For example, in the days of Gideon, the Midianite army was struck by a divinely inspired panic which caused the enemy soldiers to pick up their swords and kill one another (Jdg 7:19–22)! Or, in the time of Joshua, God made the sun stand still in the sky, so that daylight lasted long enough to allow the Israelite soldiers to kill off their opponents. In the Court History, on the other hand, there are no events which we would label supernatural or miraculous. Everything unfolds in a completely natural way that is perfectly intelligible from what we know about ordinary human interactions. Yet, as von Rad insists, the author of the Court History firmly believes that God is present and active in these events (see 2 Sam 11:27; 12:24; 17:14). What this means is that the author of the Court History developed a revolutionary new way of understanding the divine activity in history. That activity is no longer confined to the supernatural and extraordinary. On the contrary, it is precisely in and behind the fully human and perfectly ordinary course of events that God's presence is to be experienced. Thus, according to von Rad, the Court History presents a striking theological insight which is remarkably modern in its applicability.

A more recent article by J. A. Wharton is, in part at least, a further development of some of the ideas presented by von Rad.[9] Wharton points to the storyteller's ability to depict his characters as fully free and independent human beings in all their ambiguity, embodying both virtue and vice. Such honesty is possible because in a sense the real subject of the story is God's commitment to fulfill his purpose, through the establishment of Jerusalem and its anointed king, of bringing about

"the universal kingdom of his love and justice and peace."
Wharton suggests that such a theology has contemporary rel-
evance. Though our experience of life may at times appear to
be far removed from anything "godlike," we may rest assured
that in the starkest human experience, God is present in an
incredibly intimate manner and that "this hidden and intimate
Lord will never surrender us, or the purposes of his kingdom,
until the peaceable kingdom comes (p. 354)."

The most sustained effort to mine the theological ore of
the Court History and other related narratives is found in a
stimulating series of articles by Walter Brueggemann.[10] He
takes his lead from von Rad's description of the restraint with
which the author of the Court History depicts God's involvement in human events. For Brueggemann, this is essentially
a question of trust, as is most clearly reflected in 2 Sam 7 which
reports Yahweh's promise of eternal fidelity to David and his
dynasty. The king is raised up and given responsibility for the
governance of a kingdom. No detailed instruction or "law" ac-
companies this appointment: David is to enjoy freedom and
responsibility for carrying out his assigned task knowing that
he is trusted and that the trust will never be taken away. The
stories about David portray him as a person who was a bold
risk-taker in exercising this freedom, at times going against the
social expectations of his contemporaries (for example, 2 Sam
12:15–23). The astounding graciousness of God, who remains
with the chosen king in spite of gross dereliction and dismal
failure (2 Sam 12:13; 17:14), is part of the "gospel" proclaimed
by the author. This divine forbearance, however, is not the
manifestation of a cosmic laissez-faire, for when limits are
transgressed, God is there to guarantee that the human choice
of death does not thwart the divine purpose of promoting life
(e.g., 2 Sam 11:27). Moreover, the biblical material recognizes
that there are moments when the human receiver of the promise can be most free and most responsible by returning the gift

of trust and leaving certain matters in God's hands (e.g., 2 Sam 15:24–29; 16:5–13). Through all of this, David does not just represent a theology of kingship, but embodies an understanding of the relationship between God and the human person which is remarkably secular in character and particularly appropriate as a model for the contemporary world.

Before ending this overview of what kinds of questions are investigated by critical scholars when they study the Davidic Court History, a couple of observations are in order. First, it is significant to observe that theological questions such as are considered in the three above paragraphs occupy a very small portion of the published scholarly literature on the Court History. In terms of intensity and of quantity, it is clear that the attention of scholars has focused on the effort to unravel various sources or redactional stages and to link these with particular political biases. In view of this, we can only be grateful that some authors have indeed published the results of a more theological investigation. When we turn to these theological reflections, such as those of von Rad, Wharton and Brueggemann summarized above, we find what is typical of the way in which critical scholars analyze the religious ideas in biblical texts. A fundamental characteristic of such studies is that they are essentially *descriptive,* that is, they attempt to describe the theological ideas embodied in the texts independently from the personal theological beliefs of the investigator. At the same time, it is transparent to the reader that these scholars approve of and admire the religious concepts they describe—concepts of how God is present in historical events, how human freedom interrelates with God's faithful pursuance of his purpose, how trust and responsibility are characteristics of a life which is fully human and profoundly religious. Indeed it is suggested, sometimes explicitly, sometimes implicitly, that these concepts are especially commendable as a viable theological perspective for the modern world.[11] Studies such as these represent the kind of academic biblical scholarship which is most helpful in the area of personal appropriation. The ideas they contribute are valuable. Nonetheless, I believe there is still a need to go beyond the level of ideas in order to reach a more existential involvement. The next section of the chapter will describe a group process technique which opens the way to a deeper experiential contact with the narrative.

3. Experiential Group Process

It is now time to describe some of the ways in which one can work with the Court History in a more intuitive and experiential manner. I have been experimenting with these methods for several years in my introductory Old Testament course which is taught to undergraduates at the University of Dayton. The students begin by spending about two to three weeks studying the Davidic Court History from the historico-critical perspective, dealing with the kinds of questions surveyed in the previous section. On one particular occasion, this more objective phase was completed shortly before a long holiday weekend. My classes were scheduled for the last afternoon before this break, a time when attendance tends to decline. I therefore informed the students during the previous meeting that on the next class day we would be taking a very different approach to the material, looking at how it relates to our personal lives. I told them that I regarded this aspect as in some ways more important than what we had been doing so far, but that they would not be tested on what would happen that day and that attendance was optional. As it turned out, each of my two sections had eight students in attendance, an ideal number for small group process.

We began with a few minutes of brainstorming on the

characteristics of David as he is presented in the story. My purpose was simply to make sure that their knowledge of the story they had been studying was fresh in their minds. First I asked them to bring up positive qualities which led them to like David, or at least to feel positive about him as a person. Then we switched to aspects of David's personality which might be considered negative and which inclined them to dislike or disapprove of him. In the brainstorming process, they came up with about 6 to 8 features in each of the two categories.

I then told them that I wanted to lead them into a more meditative attitude in which they would allow their intuition, imagination and feeling to have free play without constant comment and censure from their rational thinking process. One way of doing this is to allow oneself to become concentrated on the awareness of bodily movement and sensation. So we did some simple movements with the understanding that we would not allow ourselves to "think" about what was going on, but simply to experience as fully as possible the physical sensation of the movement. We began by standing up and shaking our hands as if shaking off water from them. Then we let the arms, the shoulders and eventually the whole upper body get into the shaking. I teased them about the possibility that they might feel self-conscious and perhaps somewhat embarrassed at such an activity, and suggested they just shake out the self-consciousness as drops of water falling off their fingers onto the floor. Then we sat down and did slow gentle neck rolls—two or three in each direction. Always, the intent is to experience the physical sensation and not to think about what is happening, or about anything else for that matter. Sitting erect with both feet on the floor and with eyes closed, we did some slow deep breathing. I told them to allow the exhalation to take away any tension in their bodies and in fact to deliberately relax more and more each time they breathed out.

Then I said, "Let your incoming breath now take you more and more deeply within yourself, guiding you to that place where you feel free to be imaginative and creative."

In the background, I played music which sounded Oriental enough to fit the situation,[12] and asked them to imagine David on his deathbed, a scene which occurs in 1 Kgs 1. I told them to use their imaginations to bring up this scene as vividly and with as much detail as possible: the old king is at the end of his long career; he knows that he is dying; he is remembering what happened during his lifetime, especially within his own family. I suggested that they visualize what the room looks like, what David is wearing, what bed he is on, perhaps even imagining some of the smells and sounds that might be present. I then instructed them to let themselves enter into David and become David for a few minutes. "As David, you are reviewing your life as it is coming to an end. How does your life appear to you? What do you feel about your life? What images or words capture what your life has been?"

After a few minutes, I asked them to bring themselves back to the reality of the classroom in a gradual and gentle manner. We then went around the circle sharing how each had imagined David to be feeling. I then instructed them to close their eyes again for a few minutes and to try to see if they could find ways in which the feelings they had created for David in their imaginations had anything to do with the way they felt about their own lives. We then went around the circle again, reporting on the insights which each person had. I would like to illustrate, using fictitious names, what some of the students came up with.

Anne was an attractive, quiet and well-dressed young woman who was involved in a number of programs sponsored by Campus Ministry. She said that the strongest feeling David had was a sense of regret that he had made so many mistakes in his life and that those mistakes had such painful consequences for his children. What he wanted more than anything else was to somehow help his son Solomon to avoid making the same mistakes. When she related this to her own life experience, it was remarkable to see the extent to which her projection of David's feelings corresponded to what she felt about herself. She believed very strongly that the religious training she had received from her parents and her teachers contained so much distortion that it had led her to reject the Catholic tradition for a period of time. This alienation and the struggle to find a reconciliation with her religious tradition had been very painful for her. She now wants to work in the field of religious education of youngsters and try to make sure that a more adequate training will help to spare them some of the pain which she experienced. The story of David, as she created it, mirrored her own story.

A young man named Bob was a volunteer Sunday school teacher. Slightly overweight, he gave the impression of shyness and self-consciousness. He had imagined David as experiencing a great weariness from all the tasks which had been demanded of him in his life. This David looked back with nostalgia at the simple life of a shepherd from which he had been taken at such an early age. He regretted the fact that he had never been adequately prepared for the responsibilities which were thrust upon him. What Bob shared about his own life was that his mother had died when he was quite young and, as the oldest sibling, he had to assume responsibility for his brothers and sisters. This was more than he felt capable of doing. Not only did he feel burdened, but he felt sorry that he had missed out on many of the carefree good times which were enjoyed by other children his age. The connections which Bob made between David and himself were instrumental in my learning something important. As a matter of fact, the narrative of David as a young shepherd is not part of the Court History. Moreover, although the Court History has some claim to being historically factual, it can be cogently argued that the account of the young shepherd rising to the throne is a conventional motif of ancient Near Eastern literature and probably not factual. At one time in my teaching career, I would have discounted and "refuted" Bob's reconstruction of what David felt on his deathbed because it drew on a story that "was not part of the assignment" and that was probably legendary anyway. I now feel that the process which was unfolding in Bob's personal recreation of the story was of far greater significance for him, as well as for any genuine education, than the conclusions of an investigation which aims at being objective and critical.

Charlie was a big fellow who looked like a football player and who had not participated very much in class so far. He imagined David as feeling sorrow and regret for the mistakes he made and wishing he could go back and change things. Charlie informed us that he was experiencing a period of confusion about what he should major in. He wanted to go into Computer Science, but because he had "goofed off" his first two years in college, his cumulative point average was short of the minimum required to get into the major of his choice.

A young woman I'll call Denise had participated often in class discussion and often stopped to chat with me before or after class. Her theological views were more conservative and she was not very comfortable with the historico-critical method, though we were able to talk about that in an open and mutually respectful way. She thought that David had felt positively about his life, knowing that he had done the best he could in difficult situations and that was all that was necessary. After the second stage of the process she told us that earlier in her life she had experienced a great deal of negative feeling about her life. More recently, however, she had started being more gentle with herself, telling herself that she had done the best she could under the circumstances and that she did not have to put herself down anymore.

The student who expressed the strongest feelings during the exercise was Ed. He had imagined that on his deathbed, David had experienced the deepest despair because he was convinced that he had "screwed up" his entire life. The second stage of the process, in which it was suggested that what persons had imagined about David reflected their feelings about their own lives, was difficult and disturbing for Ed. He said that he had always thought of himself as being quite successful and he believed that he had a very positive self-image. However, he was able to communicate to us that on deeper reflection he could get in touch with a part of himself which told him that in spite of all the successes, he had really "screwed up" his life in those areas that counted the most. I asked Ed to think through the biblical story to see if there might be something in it that would help both him and David out of this situation. After some thought, he referred to 2 Sam 12:13 where the prophet Nathan assured David that his sin was forgiven. David's problem, thought Ed, was that he really did not *believe* in this forgiveness. In response to this, I asked the class to close their eyes again and to visualize David as a sick old man, feeling discouraged about his life because he thinks he "screwed it up." I then suggested that they open their own hearts to this David, to let love and forgiveness pour out over him; to visualize this forgiveness as a healing light streaming from their own hearts over David. "Visualize yourself walking up to him, putting your arms around him and comforting him so that he can learn to experience love, acceptance and forgiveness." I suggested that by doing this for a character in a story, a character as elaborated by our own imaginations, we can help ourselves to learn the same messages.

When my students did the first stage of the visualization process, they had no idea that they would later be asked to connect what they imagined David feeling with what they felt about their own lives. It is therefore extraordinary that such close correspondences emerged. What this demonstrates is that when we read a powerful story and let ourselves imagine creatively about it, we are really involved in a process of understanding ourselves. Getting deeply in touch with the humanity of the person in the story, we get more deeply in touch with our own humanity and have the opportunity of sharing this with one another. Moreover, as in the case of Ed, by working with the story character, we can experience healing and forgiveness in our own lives.

The issues we deal with in typical courses where classroom activity is focused on the content-material as organized by the instructor, are often very far removed from what is really going on in the lives of our students and in our own lives. The activity reported above, and others like it, reminds me of this in a powerful way. I feel very privileged to be part of a process in which students share so much of themselves. I believe that education happens in a most significant way when persons become more aware of their own life journey, choosing their own path, being empowered to move on in a trusting and joyful spirit.

4. A Variation

In a second section of the same course, I chose to do a somewhat different process with the same narrative material. As with the earlier section, we started off with the brainstorming, then used bodily movement and breathing to encourage a meditative attitude. I asked the students to continue to keep their eyes closed and to survey the plot of the story in their minds in order to select the scene in which they felt most positive about David, perhaps approving of him or admiring him. I told them to identify in their minds the quality or character trait of David which led them to have a favorable attitude towards him in this particular scene. "Now imagine the scene as vividly as possible," I continued, "see the persons present, what they look like and what they are wearing. Hear the sounds and smell the smells connected with what is going on. Imagine the quality or character trait which you feel positive about growing in David, becoming stronger and stronger until it is the guiding and dominant force in his personality and his behavior. Now let your imagination be entirely free to create a different ending to the story based on David's acting more completely in tune with the quality or characteristic you have chosen. Don't let your knowledge of what actually happened historically or what seems logically realistic tie you down or limit your creativity."

After about five minutes, I instructed them to gradually and gently bring themselves back to the reality of the classroom so that we could discuss what each had imagined about David. Then I asked them to close their eyes again and to focus on their breathing:

> Let your exhalation be a means of relaxing any physical tension in your body. Relax your shoulders and arms; release any tension in your jaw or forehead. Place any distracting thoughts on the outgoing breath and just release them. Now let your incoming breath take you into yourself, leading you deeply within. Imagine that same quality or character trait which you found in David as being present within you. Perhaps you can even feel this quality in some specific part of your body, but that is not necessary. Now with each inhalation, let that quality begin to expand within you becoming larger and stronger. Let it fill your whole body until it becomes the dominant guiding force in your life. Let your imagination feel entirely free to create what your life might become if you lived more completely on the basis of this quality.

I allowed about five minutes of silence and then called their attention back to the circle so we could hear what each had dreamed for himself or herself.

A young woman I will call Marie had started from the scene in 2 Sam 9 where David generously gave to Mephibosheth (or Meribaal) all of the property which had previously belonged to his grandfather, Saul. She imagined that this generosity grew to the point where David enjoyed giving so thoroughly that he gave away everything he owned, including the throne, and went back to being a shepherd. When she related this to herself, she said that she very much wanted to avoid getting caught up in the "rat race" of success and gaining material possessions. Her dream for herself was that she would be a giving person who did not try to hold onto security and material things but could live a free and simple life.

Greg focused on the scene in 2 Sam 16 where Shimei was throwing insults and stones at David and where David refrained from responding with violence and just let the situation be. This related to a struggle he was experiencing in his life where he observed himself repeatedly having initially judgmental and hostile reactions to people. He had visualized that if he could allow these initial feelings to just be, without acting upon them, he would make friends more easily. He would get to accept people as they are and learn to like them. Moreover, they would get a chance to know him as he really was and not get put off by his immediate negative reactions. What he imagined himself becoming was an open and loving person who experienced feelings of closeness with others.

Amy had imagined that the love which David felt so passionately for his sons became more inclusive so that it also embraced his daughter Tamar. As a result, David would not have ignored her after she had been raped by her half brother Amnon, but he would have listened to her sharing of the pain and humiliation she had experienced. Then David and Tamar would have developed a close loving relationship. After the second stage of the process, Amy acknowledged that the kind of relationship she imagined between David and Tamar was what she longed to experience with her father. Unfortunately he did not seem interested in or emotionally capable of the kind of relationship for which she had such a longing. Her dream was that he would change and that the relationship would become a reality.

It is interesting that in Amy's case, the instructions given for the visualization process were not followed exactly. Instead of imagining the quality of David growing in herself, she had visualized it growing in her father. My view is that it is perfectly all right in these intuitive processes if individuals go their own way, trusting what seems right for them. Amy centered on an issue which was obviously of great importance to her. If time had allowed, and if the setting had been somewhat different, she could have been encouraged to do some further exploration. For example, perhaps she is at the point where she has a need and the willingness to share with someone else exactly what it is in her personal experience that led her to identify so strongly with the pain and humiliation of Tamar. On the other hand, there are techniques which she could learn which would enable her to move at least in a partial manner towards the kinds of feelings she wants to have in connection with her father, even if her father never changes his attitudes or behaviors.

Finally, there is the dramatic and imaginative scenario visualized by Dan. Recalling that David had continued to love Absalom in spite of the latter's rebellion against him, Dan imagined that David continued to grow in forgiveness to the point where he forgave everyone and refused to use violence to settle issues in his kingdom. This so angered some of his advisors that they assassinated him. Afterwards, the shock of his death impressed his subjects so powerfully that they began to emulate David's forgiveness and the kingdom lived in peace without violence. In other words, Dan had his own creative way of doing what has been the consistent Christian tradition, namely seeing David as a Christ figure. In the second stage of the process, Dan saw himself as completing the study for the ministry, to which he had committed himself, and giving his life in service to others as a way of bringing about the Kingdom of God. In particular, he dreamed of teaching the path of forgiveness as a way of achieving both inner spiritual peace and a more external peace among persons who accepted one another as brothers and sisters.

The verbal sharing summarized above was of an unusual intensity. It was obvious that these students were talking about dreams which were very important for their futures. It was also clear that what they imagined for David was linked to what they hoped for in their own lives. I observed that they listened to one another quite intently and exhibited an attitude of understanding one another which I had not observed in this class before. They spontaneously affirmed and encouraged one another to believe that the dreams they had *could* be actualized in their lives.[13] For me it was a beautiful and moving experience.

NOTES

1. The traditional Hebrew text of 2 Samuel refers to this person as Mephibosheth. We know from other sources that his real name was Meribbaal. The latter, however, contains the Hebrew word *baal* which means "Lord" and came to be the common way of referring to one of the non-Israelite fertility gods. At some point in the scribal tradition, therefore, use of this term was systematically eliminated and the name of Meribbaal was deliberately distorted

into Mephibosheth which appears to mean "From the mouth of shame." This alteration was a way of casting sarcastic contempt on the god Baal. Some modern translations, such as the Revised Standard Version, stick with the Hebrew and call this man "Mephibosheth." Others, such as the New American Bible, use what was the person's real name, "Meribbaal."

2. The original work was L. Rost, *Die Uberlieferung von der Thronnachfolge Davids* (Stuttgart: W. Kohlhammer Verlag, 1926). This was reprinted in a volume entitled *Das Kleine Credo und andere Studien zum A. T.* (Heidelberg: Quelle und Meyer, 1965). Finally there is an English translation, *The Succession to the Throne of David* (Sheffield: Almond Press, 1982).

3. P. R. Ackroyd, "The Succession Narrative (so-called)," *Interpretation* 35 (1981) 383–398.

4. English language discussions of the political dimension may be found in R. N. Whybray, *The Succession Narrative* (London: SCM Press, 1968) and T. C. G. Thornton, "Solomonic Apologetic in Samuel and Kings," *Church Quarterly Review* 169 (1968) 159–166. There are more extensive discussions in German and French publications by E. Wurthwein, T. Veijola, F. Langlamet, and L. Delekat. The views of these scholars are summarized and evaluated in P. Kyle McCarter, *2 Samuel*, "The Anchor Bible" (Garden City, NY: Doubleday, 1984).

5. G. von Rad, "The Beginnings of Historical Writing in Ancient Israel," in *The Problem of the Hexateuch and Other Essays* (New York: McGraw-Hill, 1966) 166–204.

6. R. N. Whybray, *The Succession Narrative* (London: SCM Press, 1968).

7. J. Van Seters, *In Search of History. Historiography in the Ancient World and the Origins of Biblical History* (New Haven: Yale University Press, 1983) 277–292.

8. Discussion of the literary merits of the work are found in the book of Whybray referred to in note 6, above, as well as C. C. Conroy, *Absalom Absalom! Narrative and Language in 2 Sam 13–20* "Analecta Biblica" 81 (Rome: Pontifical Biblical Institute, 1978); D. M. Gunn, *The Story of King David. Genre and Interpretation* "JSOT Supplements" 6 (Sheffield: JSOT Press, 1978); and H. Hagan, "De-

ception as Motif and Theme in 2 Sm 9–20; 1 Kgs 1–2," *Biblica* 60 (1979) 301–326.

9. J. A. Wharton, "A Plausible Tale. Story and Theology in II Samuel 9–20, I Kings 1–2," *Interpretation* 38 (1981) 341–354.

10. W. Brueggemann, "David and His Theologian," *Catholic Biblical Quarterly* 30 (1968) 156–181; "The Trusted Creature," *Catholic Biblical Quarterly* 31 (1969) 484–496; "On Trust and Freedom, A Study of Faith in the Succession Narrative," *Interpretation* 26 (1972) 3–19.

11. When scholars are studying the Bible from a perspective that intends to be descriptive and they come up with theological insights which correspond with views which those scholars are already disposed to accept on other grounds, one wonders what came first. This is not to question the integrity of those scholars but to ask whether the descriptive method is really that objective. Perhaps we could frankly admit that the theological or philosophical ideas to which we are committed influence, right from the start, what we end up finding in the Bible.

12. The tape used on this occasion was *East-West Flute* available from Kripalu Center, Box 793, Lenox, MA, 01240.

13. At this point, if time had allowed, it would have been appropriate to use a process such as the one described below, pages 66–67, to heighten the sense of mutual support.

Chapter Two

"Here I Am, Lord": Our Response to the Call

One of the essential ingredients for a happy and satisfying life is having a sense of purpose or meaning. When we look at the great figures of the Old Testament, we find that their sense of purpose was based on the conviction that they had been called by God to fulfill a specific role or function which was part of God's overall interaction with Israel and the world. This experience of being called was often expressed in a special literary genre which biblical scholars have labeled the "call narrative." Reflection upon the biblical call narratives can be a highly effective way for us to get in touch with our own inner experience of how we too each have a unique call. Because of this call, our life journeys become something more than aimless wandering. They take on direction and significance.

The key to finding a relationship between the Old Testament call narratives and our own lives consists in identifying those elements or aspects of the stories which correspond with some aspect of our own individual life experience. This chapter begins with a review of the relevant narrative materials from the Old Testament. It moves on to a description of three distinct settings in which persons can explore and utilize the connections between the biblical stories and their own life process. The three settings include small groups where a high degree of interaction is possible; a series of presentations to a larger group; and a more adventuresome variation for physically active people.

1. The Narrative Material

a. The Call of Moses (Ex 3:1–4:17).   According to the Bible, Moses is the human mediator who was most intimately involved in the events of liberation, covenant-making, and law-giving which established Israel as a people. If anyone merits to be designated "founder" of ancient Israelite religion, he is the one. The story of how Moses was commissioned to carry out his task is therefore particularly significant. The material in Ex 3:1–4:17 is attributed by literary critics to the so-called J and E sources which have been put together to form a single composite account.[1] Since these sources were not written until several centuries after the time of Moses, it is reasonable to assume that the narrative is not so much an accurate historical report as the reflection of the views of later generations. In addition to the commissioning of Moses, the passage includes the account of the revelation of God's special name, "Yahweh" as well as a statement containing word-play which is intended to explain the meaning of the name (3:13–15). The precise meaning of "Yahweh" and the exact significance of the word-play are much debated topics which can be left out of consideration since they do not bear directly on the matter of the call.[2]

At the start of the account, Moses is engaged in the very ordinary activity of herding sheep and goats, an occupation by which he earns his livelihood. Then a very unusual experience interrupts his otherwise humdrum world: he sees a burning bush which is not consumed by the flames. On the one hand, his curiosity is aroused and he wants to investigate this fascinating phenomenon more closely, but on the other hand a voice tells him that the ground he is standing on is holy ground upon which he ought not to trespass unless he shows respect by removing his shoes. This two-sided reaction of attraction and awe are characteristic of the mystical encounter. Many interpreters, consequently, take the burning bush as a symbol for an inner spiritual experience rather than a factual event. Be that as it may, it is at this point that Moses is solemnly commissioned to lead his enslaved people out of Egypt into freedom. The reaction of Moses is quite surprising: he resists God's plan saying, "Who am I that I should go to Pharaoh and lead the Israelites out of Egypt?" This might seem at first to be mere polite self-deprecation. However, the true nature of his demur is made clear by the fact that it is followed by a series of three additional objections! In 4:1 the objection is that the people will not believe that he was sent by God and therefore will not listen to him. After God provides a solution to this difficulty, he comes up with another one: he is not an eloquent person but a man "slow of speech and of tongue." God rather patiently responds to this objection too. Finally, Moses tries to get out of the whole thing by saying, "My Lord, please send somebody else." At this, God angrily concedes that he will send Moses' brother Aaron along to help, but Moses can not get away from his vocation.

If the string of objections raised by Moses present a striking aspect of the narrative, the divine responses are also significant. The heart of the matter is in God's answer to the first objection, "I will be with you." The name Yahweh is based on the Hebrew verb "to be" which also occurs in the "I am" saying of 3:14. In the context of the chapter, therefore, the divine name and its explanation reinforce the "I will be with you" in a powerful manner. It is as if the text were saying that the very essence of this God is to "be with" the person called and sent on a special mission. The response to the call, therefore, requires an attitude which is identical with the fundamental religious response of the human relationship with God, namely trust (see the discussion in Chapter Three). The divine response to the second objection is somewhat different, but with the third and fourth objections, we are essentially back to the issue of trust. According to 4:11 Moses' lack of eloquence is not a problem because the Lord is the one who gives the gift of speech. Since it is God's plan which Moses is to carry out, it is inconceivable that God would not be able to provide his agent with the adequate skills to carry out his commission. Finally, in the case of the fourth objection, the divine reaction includes the statement "I will be with your mouth," which echoes the words and themes of 3:12, "I will be with you."

Though profound mystical encounters are still experienced by some people, most of us today will not experience our call in anything as dramatic as the burning bush. Nonetheless, there are other features of this narrative with which many contemporary persons will be able to identify. One of these features is the fact that the call often breaks into the ordinary day to day activity of a person's occupation, interrupting what has hitherto seemed normal and important, to send the person off in a completely new and perhaps disturbing direction. The objections raised by Moses are also representative: an inappropriate humility makes us see ourselves as unworthy; we are afraid other people will not believe in our being called; or we lack confidence that our skills are adequate to the task. In short, there is a great deal here which makes it possible for us to see the story of the call of Moses as a prototype or paradigm having more universal significance.

b. The Call of Gideon (Jdg 6:11–24).   After the death of Moses, the leadership of Israel was taken over by Joshua who led the people into the promised land which they conquered and settled. Then followed a period of about 200 years in which the form of government consisted of a tribal confederation in which the most notable figures were military leaders called "judges." One of these judges was Gideon who led his people in the struggle against a foreign power named Midian.

When Gideon experienced his call from God, he was engaged in the very mundane task of beating out wheat which he stored in a concealed place to protect it from the Midianites. Suddenly he beholds the apparition of a figure called "the messenger of the Lord." Here, as in a number of other Old Testament stories, the figure who appears is sometimes addressed as if he were God in person, and sometimes as if he were an emissary sent to represent God. This vacillation may trouble the modern reader's sense of logic and consistency, but apparently the ancient writers felt that the Lord and the Lord's messenger were so closely identified that the boundary between them was insignificant. Anyhow, the message given to Gideon is that he is to deliver his people from the power of Midian. The young man objects, "Lord, how could I deliver Israel since my clan is the weakest in Manasseh and I am the least in my family?" The reassuring response is similar to that received by Moses, "I will be with you." This is not enough for Gideon, however, and he asks for a sign. He hurries to prepare an offering of food and places it before the heavenly visitor. When the latter touches it with the tip of his staff, it goes up in a burst of fire. At this, Gideon is convinced that he has seen "the messenger of the Lord." His need for reassurance does not end here, however. As we look beyond the call narrative to the rest of the story of Gideon, the theme comes up again and again. In 6:36–40, we learn that before going into battle, Gideon comes up with a test to find out if God really intends to grant him a victory. He puts a lamb's fleece on the threshing floor telling God that the sign will be that dew is to fall on the fleece during the night but not on the ground around it. When this indeed happens, he apologetically says to God, "Let me try just one more test." This time he wants dew on the ground, but not on the fleece. This too comes to pass, but it is not the end of the story. In Jdg 7:9–18 it is God who senses Gideon's continued apprehension and tells him to sneak down to the enemy camp and see what he overhears. Spying upon the Midianites, he overhears one soldier relate a dream which symbolizes Gideon's victory. Thus reassured, he is finally ready to go into battle.

The call of Gideon has some features in common with that of Moses. In both cases, the person was engaged in very pragmatic and down to earth occupations at the time of experiencing the call. The call, then, breaks in as an interruption of their normal lives starting them out on something radically new and different. Also, both men initially object to their being selected for the task, though this particular motif is much more pronounced in the case of Moses. What distinguishes the story of Gideon is his repeated search for signs that it is indeed the Lord who is sending him and that the mission will indeed be a successful one. This uncertainty and constant need for reassurance is a feature which many contemporary readers will be able to identify with.

Finally, I would like to point to the lack of clarity about the identity of the figure who appears to Gideon. Is it the Lord or the messenger of the Lord? The ambiguity is analogous, in a loose way, to the manner in which God's call often comes in our own experience—that is, it comes through the words of another human being. It takes a particular kind of openness to acknowledge that what is said to us by another person, maybe even someone we don't like, can actually be God's word for us, the vehicle of our being called. So even this somewhat foreign ancient concept of "the messenger of the Lord" can become symbolic of an important aspect of our own experience.

c. The Call of Samuel (1 Sam 3:1–4:1).   The ministry of Samuel took place at the end of the period of the judges—a time of major transitions for the twelve Israelite tribes. The shrine at Shiloh, the central Israelite sanctuary of the time, would end up destroyed and the priestly line of Eli would be terminated. The ark of the covenant, housed at Shiloh would be captured by the Philistines and eventually brought by David to the city of Jerusalem which then became the center of national religious loyalty. And of course the institution of the judges would be replaced by a new form of political organization, the monarchy. Samuel was a central figure in all these changes and he, more than any other individual, can be said to have presided over the multi-dimensional transition period.

Samuel had been brought to the Shiloh shrine as a young boy to be trained in the religious traditions of Israel by the old priest Eli. At the beginning of 1 Sam 3, we are informed that in those days the word of the Lord was rare and that vision was not widely experienced. With this background information, the narrative goes on to speak of a particular night when Samuel, as was his custom, was sleeping in the innermost part of the shrine, the holy of holies, where the ark of the covenant was kept. He heard a voice calling, "Samuel, Samuel." Thinking that Eli was summoning him, he responded, "Here I am," and ran to the room where the old priest spent the night. But Eli said that he had not called and that the boy should go back to sleep. Twice more, the calling of his name awakened Samuel and brought him running to Eli. The third time, the priest, "whose eyesight had begun to grow dim so he could not see," perceived that the call was coming from God. He told his young charge that if it happened again, he should say, "Speak, Lord, for your servant is listening."

Sure enough, God called again, and this time Samuel knew the correct way of responding. He was able to hear as the Lord commissioned him to be a prophet. However, the first message which Samuel received that night was not one he looked forward to delivering. For the word he was entrusted with spoke of the coming end of the house of Eli in punishment for the corruption of Eli's sons who had abused the privileges of the priesthood. We can easily sympathize with Samuel's reluctance to communicate this information to his aged mentor. But the old man insisted, "What was it that he told you? Don't hide anything from me." So Samuel told him the whole thing. Eli responded with dignity and resignation, "It is the Lord. He can do whatever he thinks is right." From that time on, the Lord appeared and revealed his word to Samuel frequently and everyone in all Israel came to acknowledge Samuel's gift of mediating the word of God.

One of the most interesting features of this story is the way it deals with the problem of recognizing God's call or word when we experience it. What, for example, are we to make of the statement that "the word of the Lord was rare in those days"? Is it that God speaks more at one period of time and less at another? Or might it be the case that in fact God is always speaking, always calling, but sometimes people don't know how to hear? The events in the story suggest that the problem does indeed lie in our inability to recognize the divine summons for what it is. Samuel experiences the call three times without realizing what it is he is hearing. There is a lovely irony in the fact that it is the old blind person who is able to see what is actually taking place, whereas the young man who has physical sight, like us, can be blind to a spiritual awakening. Samuel, however, does become able to perceive once he has learned that an attitude of obedient attention ("Speak, Lord, for your servant is listening") is necessary in order to receive the divine communication.

The story also presumes that God's call does not have any special ethereal sound to it and can easily be mistaken for a merely human voice. We could take this as an indication to us that much of what we hear and experience as just a human being talking to us might actually be an embodiment of God's call which we do not "hear" because we do not know how to recognize it as God's call. A related issue arises from the fact that the story does not make it clear whether the voice came to Samuel within a dream while he slept or whether it was an external sound which he heard after being awakened by it. Whatever may be the case in this specific story, there are many other biblical narratives where a divine revelation is explicitly said to come in a dream, for example, Gen 37:5–11; 1 Kgs 3:5–14; Mt 1:18–21, among many other examples. So if it seems that the times in which we live, like the days of Samuel, are times when the word of the Lord is rare and vision is not widespread, perhaps the real problem is that we are not able to recognize God's call when it does come to us. Perhaps if we paid more attention to the whole range of our experience, from ordinary conversation to our dreams, we could learn to find there something which it would be helpful for us to hear.

One aspect of the Samuel narrative can be disturbing to the modern reader. We can become so charmed by the simple beauty of the story of a young boy hearing God's call in the night, that we are unprepared for the harshness of the message he receives. The announcement of doom over Eli's family reflects a dark, sinister element which shocks us. In fact, I have often been tempted to leave out this part of the story when I retell it. On the other hand, this uncomfortable aspect of the story can teach us something. We need to acknowledge the reality that an individual's call to begin something new often entails the end of something old. The death of the old is often felt as something painful. It sometimes involves our telling persons we love who have served as mentors, teachers and guides, that we feel called to something quite new which differs significantly from the path they wished for us to choose. Samuel serves as a good model for straightforward honesty in such situations. There will also be situations in which we find ourselves in Eli's role, watching our children, our students, and our protégés make their own choices based on their own inner guidance. From him we can learn to trust and to let go knowing that the persons we have tried to guide are now in better hands.

d. Elijah at Mount Horeb (1 Kgs 19:1–18). This passage is not technically an example of a call narrative. Nonetheless, it does include the commissioning of Elijah for specific tasks and it reflects the call narrative genre in a number of other ways too.[3]

The story takes place in the 9th century B.C. during the time of the divided monarchy. The northern kingdom of Israel was witnessing an intense religious and cultural conflict in which traditional Yahwists like Elijah opposed foreign innovations introduced by Jezebel, King Ahab's Phoenician wife. When the queen swore that she would have Elijah killed within a day's time, he became fearful and chose to run away from the threat. He got as far as Beersheba, the southern limit of Judah, the southernmost tribe. Then leaving his servant behind, he continued one day's journey into the wilderness. There he sat under a bush, so discouraged that he prayed that God would take his life away, then he lay down and went to sleep. But a heavenly messenger awakened him, offering food and water. This miraculous provisioning was repeated a second time. Then in the strength of that food he went for forty days and forty nights till he reached Mount Horeb (= Sinai) where the Lord had appeared to Moses and entered into covenant with Israel after revealing the Ten Commandments.

At Horeb, Elijah entered a cave and took up lodging there. The word of the Lord came to him asking "What do you think you're doing here, Elijah?" The question seems to embody a reproach, implying that he had no business leaving his country, his people and his assigned responsibility. Elijah responded that the whole people of Israel had abandoned the covenant with Yahweh and that he, Elijah, was left all alone and threatened with death. The text continues:

> 11 And he said, "Go forth, and stand upon the mount before the Lord." And behold, the Lord passed by, and a great and strong wind rent the mountains and broke in pieces the rocks before the Lord, but the Lord was not in the wind; and after the wind an earthquake, but the Lord was not in the earthquake; 12 and after the earthquake, a fire, but the Lord was not in the fire; and after the fire a still small voice. 13 And when Elijah heard it, he wrapped his face in his mantle and went out and stood at the entrance of the cave. (RSV).

Again the Lord asks Elijah what he is doing there and the prophet makes the same response as before. Only this time, as reported in verses 15–18, the Lord tells him, "Go, return to your path." He is to go to Damascus and anoint Hazael to become the new king of Syria. Then he is to anoint the military commander Jehu to become king of Israel, replacing Ahab and his dynasty. In addition, Elisha will be anointed to succeed Elijah in the prophetic office. These three individuals will carry on the Lord's plan. Moreover, Elijah is assured that as a matter of fact he is not the only one left who is loyal to Yahweh, there are seven thousand others who have not bowed before the statue of Baal.

The narrative of Elijah at Horeb contains a number of puzzling features which are much discussed in the scholarly literature. In particular, there is a great variety of opinions about what is signified by the contrast between wind, earthquake and fire over against the "still small voice," and about the relationship of these divine manifestations to the commission given to the prophet in verses 15–18. In spite of the disagreements among the experts, many readers have an immediate response to the "still small voice," identifying it with the inner spiritual guidance which they experience within the quietude of their own hearts. Whatever else may have been originally intended by verses 11–13, we can safely assert that one of the main points of the whole passage is to indicate that Elijah's discouragement is unwarranted. However dismal the situation may seem from external appearances, Elijah is not alone. There are 7000 other loyal Yahwists. God's cause will inexorably succeed through the human agents designated by means of the prophetic anointing. Accordingly, the reproachful question, "What do you think you're doing here?" is followed up by the command to get back where he belongs and to finish the task he has been assigned. The divine command in verse 15 begins with a phrase which literally means, "Go, return to your path," but can also be taken to imply, "Get back to your vocation."

The account of Elijah at Mount Horeb, then, is the story of a person who became fearful and depressed, so tried to run away. He went back to the very center of God's mysterious self-revelation, Mount Horeb where it had all begun, in order to find enlightenment in his time of darkness. Listening to the "still small voice" he was able to get back onto his path and continue his life work knowing that as long as he was true to his call, it was impossible for him to fail.

e. The Call of Isaiah (Isa 6:1–13).   In the second half of the eighth century B.C., more than a hundred years after the time of Elijah, the prophet Isaiah came upon the scene. He lived and worked in the city of Jerusalem, capital of the southern kingdom of Judah. The narrative of his call to the prophetic office, found in Isa 6, uses poetic imagery connected with the concept of the heavenly council. Since God was thought of as king, it was natural to imagine that he sat on a heavenly throne in a setting analogous to that of an earthly king. Like other kings, God was conceptualized as being surrounded by all kinds of royal functionaries such as messengers, servants, and advisors. In later theological terminology, these heavenly beings would be called angels. The Old Testament, however, had more picturesque ways of describing them. In some passages we read of a full-scale debate taking place in the presence of the heavenly king before He decides some important matter. These deliberations of the heavenly council are clearly portrayed in passages such as 1 Kgs 22:19–22; Job 1:6–12 and Job 2:1–7, but they are hinted at more subtly in Isaiah 6.

The first verse of the chapter introduces the vision which Isaiah received in which he saw the divine king enthroned in the temple. The seraphim, one of the groups which belong to the heavenly council, surround God while they sing, "Holy, holy, holy is the Lord, God of Hosts. The whole earth is full of his glory." The holiness of God, which elicits awesome fear and mysterious fascination, is characteristic of profound religious experiences.[4] The indication that the place shook and was filled with smoke reflects the overwhelming power of the vision. We are reminded of the Lord's revelation to Moses in smoke and earthquake on Mt. Sinai.

In reaction to this vision of God's holiness Isaiah becomes aware of his own unworthiness, symbolized by his "unclean lips." To be in the proximity of such holiness while one is in an unclean state threatens annihilation. But one of the seraphim purifies his lips, thus making him fit to stand in the divine presence. At this point, the prophet hears God ask, "Whom shall I send and who will go for us?" The plural pronoun "us" indicates that the Lord is addressing the question to the heavenly council. Before the deliberations ever get under way, however, Isaiah takes the initiative and volunteers saying, "Here I am, send me."

The task which he was assigned, however, might well

have made him regret the eagerness which he had displayed
for this role. For he is informed in verses 9–10 that his ministry
is going to lead to very negative consequences. In dismay, he
asks the Lord how long such a despairing situation will last.
The divine response offers little ground for hope, pointing instead to unremitting doom and destruction. It would be interesting to know more about how Isaiah as a person dealt with
the emotional and psychological consequences of the role he
was called upon to play. A short remark in 8:17 indicates that
all he could do was to wait in trustful expectation until this dark
period when the Lord was "hiding his face from the house of
Jacob" would come to an end.

   f. The Call of Jeremiah (Jer 1:4–10).   In the year 587
B.C., about a century after the death of Isaiah, the city of Jerusalem was conquered and destroyed by the Babylonians.
The kingdom of Judah and the dynasty of David which had
ruled it, came to an end. Thousands of people, especially the
educated, the wealthy and the powerful, were taken captive
and brought into exile to Babylonia, hundreds of miles away.
The activity of the prophet Jeremiah took place in the years
immediately preceding and following these traumatic events.
   The Lord's address to Jeremiah is brief but powerful, "I
knew you even before I formed you in your mother's belly; I
sanctified you even before you came out of the womb; I established you as a prophet to the nations." The statement that the
divine choice even preceded the prophet's birth highlights in
a way that goes beyond the earlier call narratives how thoroughly the prophet's whole existence is defined and per-
meated by the nature of his vocation. Jeremiah, however, is
not pleased by God's selection. Like Moses and Gideon before
him, he has objections. One of these objections is exactly the
same as was made by Moses, "I do not know how to speak."
Moreover, he adds, "I am a mere youth." As in the previous

cases, the Lord overrides the objection adding, "Do not be afraid of them for I am with you to protect you." Once again we are reminded of the calls of Moses and Gideon where the assurance "I am with you," is presented as a sufficient antidote to the fear of the person called. Without waiting for any sign of Jeremiah's acceptance, the Lord places his hand on the prophet's mouth saying, "Behold I have placed my words in your mouth. I have established you today over the nations and over the peoples to root up and to break down, to destroy and demolish, to build and to plant." As was the case for Samuel and Isaiah, the divine commission has a destructive aspect, but in the case of Jeremiah that is complemented by a positive aspect "to build and to plant."

The call of Jeremiah, then, clearly falls within the pattern which we have seen in earlier examples of the genre. The principal element of originality is found in the claim that God's election of the person preceded his birth. The passage is also striking in the very graphic symbol of God's hand touching the mouth in order to put his words there. We are of course dealing with a poetic image, but one which treats the word of God as a physical and tangible reality.

Commentators have frequently pointed to the interesting contrast between Isaiah's eagerness to offer himself for the role of prophet and Jeremiah's objection that he is too young and inexperienced for the task. The historical reason for this difference is difficult to ascertain. Nonetheless, as we reflect upon our own experience we can perhaps identify persons who according to temperament are more like Isaiah in this regard while others are more like Jeremiah. In fact, even within the life of a single individual, there are probably times in which we have eagerly taken on a task and other times in which we would have gotten out of it if we could. To that extent, the stories of these prophets reflect typical human experiences.

The reluctance with which Jeremiah took on the prophetic vocation seems to be justified by the eventual course of his career. We possess more biographical information about him than about any other prophet. What that information reveals is that he led a lonely life marked by constant conflict and repeated persecution at the hands of his enemies. A number of passages in the book of Jeremiah contain his complaining dialogue with God. Full of inner turmoil and poignancy, these "Confessions of Jeremiah" reveal as no other biblical passages, the doubt and pain which can mark the lives of persons who strive to be faithful to the call they have received.[5]

g. The Call of Ezekiel (Ezek 1–3).   Ezekiel was apparently among the captives deported to Babylon in 597 B.C. There he received his call and announced the destruction of the temple which took place in 587. After those disastrous events he continued to preach to the exiles and contributed important ideas to the movement which would result in the restoration of the Jewish community in Jerusalem and Judah some fifty years later.

The description of the divine manifestation or theophany takes a more elaborate form in Ezekiel than in any of the other call narratives. Four heavenly beings, with four faces each, form a fiery throne upon which the Lord is seated. The "wheels within wheels" found beneath the four living creatures symbolize the mobility of the throne. This device is used in one of Ezekiel's visions (10:1–22 and 11:22–25) to explain how God's presence was removed from the Jerusalem temple immediately prior to its destruction: the "glory" of the Lord moved from the sanctuary to the fiery throne chariot which served to take it away. In the detailed call narrative of Ezek 1–3, the throne chariot serves as a way of dealing with another theological problem. The other prophets had received their calls on Israelite territory, the land of Yahweh. Ezekiel claimed to receive his call on foreign soil. The moveable throne is Ezekiel's symbolic way of stressing that Yahweh is not tied down to any specific place. The Lord goes wherever He wants to go in order to appoint his messengers.

Although the description of God's moveable throne is much more elaborate than what appears in other call narratives, many of the individual features of the strange vision are standard elements of other accounts of the theophany. For example, the four living creatures with four faces and four wings may be thought of as representatives of the heavenly council around God's throne comparable to the seraphim of Isa 6. The fire, wind, clouds, and thunderous noise occur in varying combinations in the burning bush (Ex 3), the descent of Yahweh on Mt. Sinai (Ex 19), the experience of Elijah on Mt. Horeb (1 Kgs 19) as well as in other related texts. Ezekiel's experience, therefore, is not as idiosyncratic as may at first appear to be the case.

The actual commissioning of the prophet emphasizes the overwhelming power of God's spirit, the resistance Ezekiel will encounter from the people to whom he is being sent, and his responsibility to carry out his assignment faithfully, whether he is listened to or rejected. His reception of God's word is symbolized by a scroll which he is given to eat and which tastes sweet in his mouth. The account does not contain an explicit "objection" similar to those found in some of the other call narratives. However, the fact that God warns him not to be afraid (2:6) or rebellious (2:8) may be taken as implying his resistance, or at least as intended to forestall it. The divine assurance is expressed in a threefold "Be not afraid" in 2:6 which is reminiscent of the same injunction in the call of Jeremiah.

h. The Call of Second Isaiah (Isa 40:1–8). The material contained in chapters 40 to 55 of the book of Isaiah was not composed by the prophet whose call was narrated in chapter

6 and discussed above. That Isaiah lived and preached in the last part of the 8th century B.C. Chapters 40–55, on the other hand, are the work of an anonymous prophet who, around 550 B.C., delivered a message of hope and consolation to the Judaeans who had been exiled to Babylon. Since this poet's name is not known, the convention has arisen of referring to him as Second Isaiah.

The account of Second Isaiah's call in 40:1–8 uses the concept of the heavenly council, but in a more complex manner than we have seen so far. The opening injunction is formulated with a plural verb which the King James Version translated "Comfort ye, comfort ye my people." This command, therefore, is not addressed to the prophet himself but to a group. It makes sense to take the individuals to whom the order is addressed as members of the heavenly council, heavenly messengers whom later theology would call "angels." Then in verse 3, a "voice" in the council issues orders to another group (plural imperative again), "In the wilderness prepare the way of the Lord, make straight in the desert a highway for our God (RSV)." This verse refers to a road joining Jerusalem and Babylon upon which God would appear to lead his people back home.

In verse 6, another voice in the heavenly council gives the command, "Cry." This time the verb is a singular imperative and the prophet recognizes that he himself is finally being addressed. So he responds, "What shall I cry?" Then he is given his inaugural message:

> All flesh is grass,
>> and all its beauty is like the flower of the field.
> The grass withers, the flower fades,
>> when the breath of the Lord blows upon it.
> The grass withers, the flower fades;
>> but the word of our God will stand for ever (RSV).

The thrust of the message must be seen in terms of the context to which it was addressed. The exiles might well feel disheartened in the apparent hopelessness of their situation. World events seemed to be controlled by great world powers like Babylonia and Persia compared to which the small conquered kingdom of Judah was completely insignificant. How then could there be any chance of their restoration? The prophetic message proclaims that great political and military power ("all flesh") is nothing to God. The real power is in the word of God, which stands for ever, and which has guaranteed that God's people will not be forsaken.

The message of Second Isaiah, then, is one of hope and consolation during times of dark despair. The prophet's voice in proclaiming this message is vastly magnified when it is realized that at the same time as he was commissioned, a whole host of heavenly comforters was sent out to do their work alongside him. Though it may not yet be apparent to merely earthly eyes, the road on which the prisoners will return is already being constructed. Many modern readers find the positive, optimistic perspective of Second Isaiah a welcome relief from the message of doom which is so much a part of other prophets such as (First) Isaiah, Jeremiah, and Ezekiel. This contrast in the tone of the different prophetic books vividly illustrates that the proclamation of the prophets did not consist of presenting abstract and timeless verities, but the announcing of a specific word which responds to the needs of a specific historical situation.

i. Third Isaiah (Isa 61:1–4). Chapters 40–55 of Isaiah exhibit such a high degree of internal consistency that we may confidently view them as the work of one author. Such is not the case for chapters 56–66 which give signs of being a miscellaneous collection from various sources. Nonetheless, it has become the convention to refer to chapters 56–66 as "Third

Isaiah." Within this collection of poems, the section 61:1–4 may be considered as a call narrative. It is an especially interesting one because it was quoted by Jesus in reference to his own mission (Lk 4:16–20; cp. Lk 7:22 and Mt 11:5). The passage speaks for itself:

> The Spirit of the Lord God is upon me,
> > because the Lord has anointed me
> to bring good tidings to the afflicted;
> > he has sent me to bind up the brokenhearted,
> to proclaim liberty to the captives,
> > and the opening of the prison to those who are bound;
> to proclaim the year of the Lord's favor,
> > and the day of vengeance of our God;
> > to comfort all who mourn;
> to grant to those who mourn in Zion—
> > to give them a garland instead of ashes,
> the oil of gladness instead of mourning,
> > the mantle of praise instead of a faint spirit;
> that they may be called oaks of righteousness,
> > the planting of the Lord, that he may be glorified.
> They shall build up the ancient ruins,
> > they shall raise up the former devastations;
> they shall repair the ruined cities,
> > the devastations of many generations (RSV).

2. Workshop with a Small Group

The Old Testament call narratives, used within a small group of 8 to 12 persons, can provide a powerful and effective means of helping persons become more aware of their own sense of being called. In such a setting, the group leader can recount each of the stories, reading some parts from the Bible and paraphrasing other parts. After each story, one asks the

simple question, "What is there in this story that you can identify with?" The objective is not to look for interesting problems
of exegesis which would stimulate our intellectual curiosity,
but to begin finding connections between the stories and our
own lives.

There are groups in which participants already have a degree of self-awareness and a willingness to share their observations in discussion. With this kind of group, the role of the
facilitator is very simple for the relevant points are spontaneously brought out. Where the contributions are not easily
forthcoming, it is possible to make suggestions and ask further
questions. For example, in connection with the story of Moses
and the burning bush, one can ask, "Did you notice how
Moses objected that he was not talented enough for the task
to which God was calling him? How many of you have felt
drawn to some service or project but weren't sure you had the
necessary skills?" Many of the hands will go up because this is
such a widespread experience. With the Gideon story I ask,
"See how Gideon just can't feel sure enough that it is really
God calling him and so he has to keep looking for reassurance
to satisfy his uncertainty. How many of you have had an experience like that?" Then with the Elijah story, if there are still
no volunteers for sharing, I talk a bit about my understanding
of the "still small voice." I speak of it as an inner voice as opposed to what we learn from books, experts and other external
teachers. I point out that this voice is quiet and subtle and can
easily be drowned out by our own busy activity. It requires
careful attention and listening. Then I tell a personal story
about an occasion when I received guidance from my "still
small voice." Afterwards I ask, "How many of you know what
I'm talking about because you experience something like this
in your own life?" This time when hands are raised it is usually
possible to get someone to share a little about their own experience of this inner voice.

Getting a group to move towards a more open sharing of their inner experiences sometimes takes a lot of gentleness and patience. It is helpful if the facilitator models the desired behavior by doing a lot of honest, open self-disclosure. The benefits which result once the sharing begins are well worth the effort. Many of us have a tendency to minimize or even discount our inner religious experience. We think, "That is just something silly about me which nobody else would appreciate." By telling about the experience to others, we give our inner realities an existence in the outside world. We learn that other people have experiences like this too, and we are not strange or alone. Moreover, we begin to see a depth in other persons which we had perhaps not suspected because we thought of them only in terms of their "outer lives" as we had observed them. The process of communication, then, helps us to respect and honor our own inner experience. No longer taking it lightly, we are more apt to hear and follow our own call.

Through discussion, people begin to see in the call narratives reflections of their own lives, their own stories. After a number of the biblical passages have been reviewed (it is not necessary to go through all of the ones summarized earlier in this chapter), I suggest that each person select one biblical call account with which he or she can most strongly identify. I then ask them to re-write the biblical story in such a fashion that it reflects their own experience of being called. Or, to put it another way, write the story of your own call following the form of the biblical stories. A participant in one of my workshops rewrote the call of Samuel in the following way:

> I was sound asleep in the temple of my own life. God's word was unfamiliar to me in those days. I heard a voice calling my name. Something inside me said, "It's just a dream. Go back to sleep." It called again and again. Finally, a part of me which was growing old and almost blind

said, "Maybe it is God calling." After that I listened and heard. From the ark, in the holy of holies, deep within, I recognized whose call it was and responded, "Here I am." Something old had to pass away, but something new was being born. And now, one step at the time, I am learning to walk my path.

An interesting feature of this person's creative retelling of 1 Sam 3 is that many elements of the story which are external realities in relation to Samuel (temple, ark, Eli) have become symbols of inner realities (the temple within, a part which "was growing old and blind"). Another person wrote a story which combines elements from the calls of Moses and Jeremiah as well as the account of Elijah on Mt. Horeb:

I searched for God in the thunder of war and the lightning of battle, but God was not there. I searched for God in the fire of business and the whirlwind of success, but God was not there. Then, in the small quiet voice of a book and the warm, loving voice of friends, God was there. I turned aside from my life and said, "I will investigate this wonderful thing," and I heard God say, "Stay here, this is holy ground." But I answered, "What can I do, I am a spiritual youth, and I have no talents. I'm here, give me a sign. Speak, Lord, your servant is listening." But the thunder, and the fire and the whirlwind are very loud and they often drown out the quiet voice. But God's voice is persistent and despite my objections, He will be heard. Then I will rebuild the old me and begin to raise up a new city of God.

About a year later, this person revised the story in a way which reflected the distance he had travelled on his journey. For the last three sentences of the first version, he substituted the following:

But the thunder and the fire and the whirlwind were very loud, and they drowned out the quiet voice, and I heard only my own voice. But the small, quiet voice would not be stilled, and it became louder and louder until it drowned out the other sounds and it became the only sound and God said, "Come, follow me." Now I will rebuild the old me, and begin to raise up a new city of God.

Another exercise which I use in a small group is one which aims at simulating an experience of being called in the actual context of the group. I use this only after enough work has been done for participants to get to know one another and feel comfortable with an activity which might seem a little risky. The room is darkened and the chairs arranged in a circle. In the center of the circle there are two candles about two feet apart. One at a time, group members step into the circle, between the candles. The other participants slowly chant that person's name five times. I simply use the one and one half step interval from C down to A and we practice a little beforehand so we can fit whatever number of syllables are necessary into that pattern.

This exercise of being called can be very powerful. On one occasion, a young man reported that he was not sure what to expect as he stepped into the space between the candles. But when the chanting started he felt that a host of angels was calling him. He said that the spiritual aspect of his life, which he had somewhat neglected, was being invited to blossom out in the company of the heavenly choirs which sang in the story of Isaiah (Isa 6:2–3). One woman said that she had felt very scared when her turn came and as she walked towards the center of the circle. However, as soon as the chanting started she felt an incredible sense of peace descend upon her. From this she concluded that perhaps her fear about her personal call was unwarranted and that if she opened herself up to hearing it, the fear would go away and she would be able to respond in a calm and peaceful manner. During the discussion after this exercise, people frequently report that their involvement in calling others by chanting the name was just as significant for them as being in the center of the circle, because they felt they were really part of calling their brothers and sisters out of themselves and into the service of the community.

Whenever I lead this exercise, I always take my own turn at being called. On one such occasion I had an interesting and unexpected experience. It became clear to me that the group of people with which I was working was genuinely calling me to do the work in which I was engaged. This surprised me at first because on the surface of things I was the one who had thought up this workshop on the call narratives. I was the one who had researched the stories, gotten people to come, and led the exercise. In spite of all that, it seemed at the time, and I now believe this is the truth of the situation, they were the ones calling me to do the work. My process of becoming more fully myself, of using my knowledge and skills to help others, of responding to my own "still small voice" is intimately inter-woven in a vaster fabric which I can not comprehend but for which I am grateful.

By this point in the workshop, most of the participants have a pretty good idea of what it is they feel called to. In order to concretize that understanding, I make art materials available and ask them to draw or paint a symbolic representation of that call. The picture can be very simple and they will not have to show it to anyone else if they don't want to. When the art work is complete, I remind them that many of the great personages of the Old Testament resisted the call because they felt some sort of inadequacy. With this in mind they are to look at the picture they have produced and see if they can become aware of what it is they think they are *lacking* and which they therefore *need* in order to move towards what they want to become.

Later, the group is seated on chairs which are arranged in a circle. In the center is a vase of cut flowers, or some other token gifts, sufficient in number so each member of the group can receive one. We go around the circle, all taking a turn explaining what their sense of call is at this point in their lives, showing the picture they made if they wish. Then they share what it is they believe they need in order to be able to respond to the call. At this point, I ask the other group members whether one of them can help supply this need. If there is no spontaneous response, I make suggestions about how the need might be met and eventually someone does respond. (If it would ever happen that nobody responded to my suggestions, I would do so myself.) The person who offers to help fill the need presents a flower as a symbol of that gift. For example, one participant may say that she is in need of much more self-confidence in order to answer her call. Another group member might react by saying, "I have known you for many years and I have loads of confidence in your ability. Take this flower as a symbol of my confidence in you and let it help you become more confident in yourself." The need which is articulated may involve the obtaining of information or the development of a skill which another participant is willing to provide. If the need is not something that anybody in that group is able to give, probably there will be a member of the group who is willing to pray for that intention on a regular basis. Sometimes, as the process gains momentum in the group, it happens that the gift which is offered does not correspond exactly with the need that was expressed. One time, for example, an older man expressed all kinds of reservations about his ability to answer his call. A group member who had not even known him before the workshop spontaneously presented him with a flower saying,

"Bill, you are such a beautiful person and I don't think you even realize how beautiful you are. Take this flower as a symbol of the wondrous beauty we all see in you."

As a result of this exercise, persons end the workshop with a concrete symbol of what it is they feel called to and an awareness of what obstacles they need to overcome. They have taken important steps by releasing their dreams from the confinement of secrecy and giving them external reality by drawing and by verbal sharing. Moreover, they have experienced acceptance and support from other people and are thus empowered to move forward in their life journeys. It is not unusual for people to report, many months later, how they and others have grown and changed since the first steps they took during this workshop.

3. Speaking to a Larger Group

The Old Testament material on the call can also be adapted for presentation to larger audiences. In that case, however, the discussion and small group processes described above are virtually impossible to implement. In such cases, it is my practice to present the content in lecture format and to use guided imagery as the principal experiential component. For example, in one of the lectures I might present the story of Elijah at Mt. Horeb. This would include discussion of the "still small voice" of our intuitive inner guidance. I give examples from my own life and check to see that people in the audience understand from their own experience what it is I am talking about. Afterwards I move on to the story of Samuel emphasizing how it deals with the problem of identifying God's call when it comes to us. I point out that it is Eli, the blind old priest, who is able to discern that it was God who was calling Samuel's name.

The above information provides the background for an exercise in guided imagery. I inform the audience that in this exercise I will use the designation "Wise Teacher" which they can interpret in whatever way they wish. It just stands for anyone who is a manifestation of wisdom, kindness, acceptance and understanding. They could take it to be the priest Eli from the story of Samuel, but it would be better to have an identification with someone they are personally familiar with. That may be a woman or a man, real or imagined. Perhaps it is an actual teacher one has had, or Jesus, or a guardian angel. Whatever fits for each individual will be appropriate. I then say something like the following:

> I would like you to sit straight, with both feet on the floor and your hands comfortably on your lap. Try to keep your back straight. Please close your eyes now and let them remain closed for the duration of the visualization. Take a few deep breaths, and as you exhale, allow your body to relax. Allow your facial muscles—eyebrows, forehead, tongue and jaw—to completely relax, dropping all expression from your face. Let your shoulders and arms hang loosely. Release the tension in your stomach muscles. Let your thighs, legs and feet relax too. With each exhalation, feel yourself moving into deeper and deeper levels of relaxation and calmness. If any thoughts enter your mind, gently release them, allowing them to float out on your outgoing breath. Also let go of whatever nervousness or whatever expectations you might have about this imagery process.
>
> Now imagine a place where you enjoy walking by yourself in order to reflect or meditate. It may be a garden or a wooded area or any other place that seems comfortable and familiar to you. Allow yourself to be fully there in your imagination, seeing, hearing, feeling and smelling the features of the place as vividly as possible. As you are walking along, you are thinking about your personal work

during the segment of your life journey which you are now entering. Think of the word "work" as broadly as possible. It's not just your job, but all the significant things you do in your life. (Pause) Walking along you see a figure up ahead who seems to be waiting for you. As you get closer you see it is the Wise Teacher who is just delighted that you have come along because he/she has been expecting you. The Wise Teacher asks you to share with him or her what you have been thinking about. Take a minute or two to do that. (Pause) Now the Wise Teacher asks, "Is there some aspect of what you have described that is especially important to you? Or is there something additional which you haven't even mentioned yet? Something you feel especially drawn to, that is close to your heart, that you dream of and wish you had time and energy to accomplish? It may be something hidden within you as a deep longing." Tell the Wise Teacher about this. (Pause) Now, if there is some question you want to ask the Wise teacher, go ahead and ask it, expecting that you will receive an answer. (Pause) Now say goodbye to the Wise Teacher, knowing that you can meet again any time you want to. After you have finished, bring yourself back to the reality of this room and open your eyes.

The visualization just described can lead to a profound experience. It often reminds persons of a call which they feel very deeply but which lies dormant in the secrecy of their inner hearts. The imagery process encourages them to bring the inner sense into heightened awareness and to begin paying more attention to it. Sometimes there may be some discomfort or even pain accompanying the awareness. Individuals become conscious that they have neglected something which is very important to them. They may feel that they are wandering very far from the path they want to be on. It may appear virtually impossible to overcome all the obstacles which are keeping them from answering this call. I therefore find it advisable to talk explicitly to the group about the possibility of experiencing painful moments. However, the call we receive from God is never in opposition to our own deepest and most intimate longings for ourselves. It is a call to "come home" to a place where we will find true serenity and inner peace. We also have to learn to be gentle with ourselves, allowing the process of our lives to unfold according to its own inner timetable. We are in a process of learning, a process of growing. To trust that process is to trust God, knowing that we will be safe along the way and that God will bring us to the fullness of who we are meant to be.

It is also a good idea for people to do some kind of follow up on the visualization experience. Perhaps the best place to start is to share the experience in conversation with another person. This is a way of honoring ourselves and valuing our experience, allowing a seed to begin to grow. If the verbal sharing is not possible, or if it seems too hard, a person could just write about the experience in a journal or notebook. One could also express the sense of call in a drawing or perhaps re-write one of the biblical stories in the manner described above (pp. 62–64).

In a subsequent meeting with the same group, I review the accounts of the calls of Moses, Gideon and Jeremiah which are summarized above (pp. 42–46, 54–56). I emphasize the series of objections which these individuals raised in their resistance to accepting God's call. On the basis of those examples it is possible to outline the typical kinds of resistance which we offer to our being called: an inappropriate humility which claims we are not worthy; fear of how other people will react to us and worry about whether they will accept our ministry; and fear that we are inadequate to the task and lack the required skills. Most people will be able to see that they have used at least one of these ways in order to place obstacles in their own path. It is important that we verbalize these obstacles in such a way that we take responsibility for them and not blame other people or situations. For example, the obstacle is not, "My friends will criticize me," but, "I am afraid of criticism," or, "I don't want to face up to the criticism." Another example would be in a case where there doesn't seem to be adequate funding for the project we want to implement. Instead of saying, "There isn't enough money," or, "They won't fund the proposal," we could take responsibility by saying, "I am fearful about the availability of funding," or, "I don't want to invest the energy that would be required to raise the money." This awareness provides the basis for another encounter with the Wise Teacher.

Once again, I lead the group through the breathing and relaxation process, asking them to return to that place where they meet with the Wise Teacher. Then I say:

Take a few moments to tell the Wise Teacher about any new insights you may have had about your call since the last time you were together. (Pause) Also tell the Wise Teacher about the resistance and the obstacles which you place in the path of answering your call. (Pause) As you are speaking, look into the eyes of the Wise Teacher and notice how loving and accepting he or she is. The Wise Teacher does not judge you for having these resistances. In fact the Wise Teacher asks, "Is there one of these obstacles which you are ready to let go of? I would like you to make a present of it and give it to me." Keeping your eyes closed, hold your hands out in front of you, palms up, as if you were holding something. Visualize right there in your hand some concrete symbol of the obstacle you are going to give away. Then slowly see your hands move towards the Wise Teacher. At the same time the Wise Teacher's hands move towards you. See the gift being transferred from one pair of hands to the other. And you notice as your resistance enters the hands of the Wise

Teacher it begins to turn into something of great beauty,
radiating a warm golden light. Looking at the Wise Teacher's eyes again, you see that he or she is perfectly delighted with your gift and so happy to have it. The Wise
Teacher says, "This is something which you received because you needed it for a time, but now you are ready to
give it back." Now the Wise Teacher goes away, carrying
your gift and you are left by yourself for a while. Experience how it feels to be without this obstacle. (Pause) See
if you can think of some ways in which you might behave
differently now that you have let go of some of your resistance. (Pause) Perhaps you are ready right now to choose
to take a concrete step towards answering your call and
becoming who you were meant to be. It can be a very
small step if that is all you are ready to handle. If you want
to, make a commitment to yourself right now to take that
step. (Pause) After you have finished with this, bring yourself back to the reality of this room, and when you are
ready, gently open your eyes.

After this exercise, I ask people to raise their hands if they
were able to identify and let go of some resistance during the
visualization process. I also ask for a show of hands if persons
felt they were holding on and just couldn't let go of the resistance. Usually there are some in each category and it is helpful
for individuals to realize that they were not alone in the reactions they had to that part of the exercise. I suggest to those
who were able to let go that they might try practicing this visualization on a regular basis until they really feel that they are
completely free of the resistance in question. The others need
to hear that holding on is just a phase in a process and that
although they are not quite ready yet to let go, it will come
eventually. We have to be patient with ourselves and allow our
inner process to unfold gradually.

I like to end this workshop or series of presentations with

an activity that creates an awareness of the community aspect of our answering of the call. One way to do this is to ask all persons to formulate the step they are moving towards in words which they would be comfortable sharing with other people in the group. Some examples would be as follows: "This year I am going to bring more personal warmth to the administration of our office"; "I am going to sign up to take the first course in the degree program I've been wanting to undertake"; "I'm going to volunteer one night a week in a community service program." I make it quite clear that if their goal is something private, they could word it very vaguely, for example, "I am going to improve my relationship with someone in my life," or, "I'm going to make a phone call I have been putting off." Then everybody stands up and mills around in cocktail party fashion. Each person finds a partner and, in just one sentence, tells the partner about the call he or she experiences or the step he or she is going to take. The other person responds with a one-sentence expression of support such as, "I support you in achieving your goal," or, "I will support you through my prayers." The two persons then exchange roles and repeat the process. They can conclude with a handshake or a hug if that seems appropriate and then move on to other partners. Participants have to be informed at the beginning that they should make it brief and keep moving around from partner to partner. After sufficient time has elapsed, all can stand in a circle and sing an appropriate hymn. I like to use "Great Things Happen When God Mixes with Us" from the hymnal *Glory and Praise*.

If the meeting is going to be followed by a celebration of the Eucharist, then another concluding activity might be tried. Each group member needs to be provided with some kind of token which represents to him or her the role or objective to which he or she feels called. These tokens should all look basically alike. It is also better if the participants have some hand in making them. One suggestion is to obtain small plastic boxes (about one inch square) which can be purchased inexpensively in variety gift shops. A pinch of small stars or decorative glitter can be placed in the box which is then tied with a colorful ribbon. These can be assembled at a stage in the workshop which will encourage each group member to identify the token with his or her call. These tokens are brought to the liturgy and at the handshake of peace, each time two persons exchange the peace, they exchange tokens. After exchanging with several people, no one will know which is which. Persons are then instructed to take home the token they ended up with. It will serve to remind them of their own token and their own call. They will also be aware that members of the community have entrusted some aspect of their call to one another and that a part of them is out there in the community. They can also be encouraged to pray for the person whose token they ended up with, asking God that the person in question receive help in responding to the call he or she has received.

4. For the Active Set

Recent developments in the holistic health field highlight the complex interconnections among the physical, intellectual, emotional and spiritual components of the total human organism. On the one hand, diseases which used to be thought of as purely physical in causation are now seen to involve emotional and spiritual factors. On the other hand, new psycho-technologies are discovering that "body work" can help persons move through emotional impasses which could not be talked out in traditional psychotherapy. It seems that emotional experiences remain stored for long periods of time in the muscular system and that the body "remembers" and "understands" one's psychological past in ways which are not always accessible to the conscious thought process. As far as the spiritual is concerned, Eastern traditions such as yoga and tai chi have long recognized that physical discipline can be conducive to religious growth. That the physical and emotional are linked to the spiritual is also reflected by Western customs such as fasting, as well as by the rich artistic traditions of Catholic and Orthodox liturgy. Consequently, there is ample precedent for suggesting that physical involvement of the body might be an appropriate way to explore the significance of certain biblical texts. The story of Elijah at Mt. Horeb is admirably suited for exploring this possibility.

Elijah, first of all, was a celebrated runner. On one occasion he outran King Ahab's horse-drawn chariot from Mt. Carmel to Jezreel, a distance of many miles (1 Kgs 18:46). It is not said explicitly that he ran all the way to Mt. Horeb, though it is stated that he "went," apparently non-stop, for forty days and forty nights without stopping to eat (1 Kgs 19:7–8). Elijah had a reputation for being "carried off" by the spirit of God so that people could not find him (1 Kgs 18:12). The fact that he went up into heaven in a chariot of fire (2 Kgs 2:11) even provided the title for a movie about running. But Elijah was not only a man who ran. He was also a man who ran away. That is something even those of us who are not runners can identify with.

The following exercise is one which I conduct only with persons who are in appropriate physical condition. Even at that, I instruct participants (who have been asked to bring running shoes for this session) to use their own judgment as to whether they should run, jog/walk, or just walk. If they exercise regularly, I recommend that they give themselves a good workout. We all go outside (an indoor track would also be okay) and run or walk separately for about ten minutes. I suggest that during the first half of that time, individuals tell themselves repeatedly, "I am Elijah. I'm running away. I feel threatened and afraid. I'm all alone. I feel so discouraged. I must get to Mt. Horeb. I have to find some answers." During the second half of the running, they are to switch to their own names concentrating especially on any phrase which may seem particularly powerful for them.

At a pre-arranged signal, we gather together again. In the background there is music with a rapid beat and we keep running or walking in place with eyes closed. I tell the group that they are now approaching Mt. Horeb and beginning to go up its slopes. In the distance they see the cave. Then they reach the cave and stoop to enter it. I have previously instructed them that the cave will have a low ceiling and they will have to stoop way down with their knees bent and buttocks almost touching the floor while in the cave. The pose is deliberately intended to be a little uncomfortable. I then say:

> Now that you are in the cave, you are safe. In your imagination, slowly turn around and look out of the cave. There you will see a symbol of what you have been running away from. Just allow the symbol to come to you. Note what the symbol is, and afterwards let it move on and go away. (Pause) Now the Lord is going to pass by. You hear and feel an incredibly powerful wind which can tear rocks off the mountain. (Appropriate background music is played for the wind, quake and fire.) But the Lord is not in the wind. The earthquake now begins. It shakes the whole mountain. Let your body shake with it. (Pause) But the Lord is not in the earthquake. Finally, there is a roaring, raging fire blazing around the whole mountain. Feel its heat and its fury. (Pause) But the Lord is not in the fire. And now, you hear the still small voice. Listen very carefully and expect to hear what you need to hear and it will come to you.

At this point, all lie flat on the floor with their heads cradled in their arms. A simple, gentle flute is playing in the background. After about five minutes I tell them that whenever they are ready they can come back to sit in a circle and we will talk about what we all experienced.

I find that this exercise is particularly effective in helping persons become more aware of what it is they are running away from. The symbols which they "see" outside the cave are sometimes what they expected to see, sometimes surprising. In either case most persons are able to recognize upon reflection that the symbol which came to them relates to something significant in their lives. The messages which participants hear in the still small voice are usually simple ones which might seem on the surface to be mere truisms of spirituality. But in this context they can have an impact which they have not had before. The matters which come up in this exercise are particularly suited for journal work. The following example is quoted in full (the person's name has been changed):

> She was afraid and fled from the dark cloud. As she reached Mt. Horeb, the cloud slowed down and waited patiently. It knew that she would check it out again.
>
> As she went into the cave, Marie went to the farthest wall and timidly looked out. But she didn't see anything. All she could do is wonder why God was doing all this in her life. It wasn't a good time—the beginning of her last year at school, etc.
>
> Then all of a sudden . . . the overwhelming wind in her head went beserk . . . everything kept playing back at her. The confusion of all of it had her emotions whipping around. Still, when she looked out of the cave, she saw nothing and went back to the far wall.
>
> Her stomach began rolling like rocks down a mountainside during an earthquake. Marie knew that the journey was just beginning and she clutched her legs and tried

to go back to her mother's womb where she had been safe and secure. As she peeked outside the cave again—she saw nothing.

But wait . . . in the distance was that black cloud that had been hovering around since she began this latest part of the journey. She ran to the back of the cave and tried to melt into the wall—she knew that within that cloud, God was giving her a message. She closed her eyes, but all she could see was the cloud with the message.

Marie saw what it was that she didn't want to acknowledge. God had been leaking it out a little at a time because of her great fear.

The cloud waited patiently and Marie finally opened her eyes and sensed the patient waiting. Then she talked with the cloud—the image that was in the midst of it became more clear. It was a woman who was in the position of being open and receptive. This same position is one of giving birth too. At this point, Marie is at a loss. She knows of the desire to be open and to be vulnerable but the pain involved in giving birth scares her. There is a deeper desire though—the desire to bring forth new life; the desire to watch as a child develops within her body so to bring it into life.

As the cloud begins to leave, Marie asks, "What do I do now?" The cloud just encloses her and murmurs, "Let go, nothing will happen, be at peace—relax, let go, be at peace."

After resting within the cloud, Marie began to go back to the "real world" and back to school. But all this she ponders in her heart. She knows that she'll need to go back to the cave again.

This account contains many rich symbols (the dark cloud, the woman in the cloud, the cave, the womb, giving birth, the child, the journey, the wall) which often appear in myths and in dreams. The depth of these images reflects the importance of the issues which this young woman is dealing with. Fortunately, it is not the responsibility of the facilitator to give an explanation of the symbols, but to provide a supportive environment in which the person can do her own work. The report shows that she is in fact quite capable of interpreting her own experience. It is interesting to see how this woman's visualization did not exactly follow what I had suggested. In her case the image of what she was running away from did not "go away," but, on the contrary, became the source of the message of the still small voice. In fact, it appears that the specific sense in which her understanding has taken some steps forward is that she became able to look at the cloud and even allowed it to enfold and comfort her. She has made progress in her self-understanding and also knows that she has more to learn. The story of a turning-point in Elijah's life has become a means of illuminating and furthering her own life journey.

NOTES

1. For an explanation of the various sources of the Pentateuch (J, E, D and P) see my book *In and Out of Paradise* (Ramsey, NJ: Paulist Press, 1983) 4–6.

2. A helpful survey of scholarship on these questions is found in the commentary on Ex 3 in B. S. Childs, *The Book of Exodus* (London/Philadelphia: Westminster Press, 1974).

3. So also M. Newman, "The Prophetic Call of Samuel," in *Israel's Prophetic Heritage*, ed. B. W. Anderson and W. Harrelson (New York: Harper & Brothers, 1962) 86–97. For a useful discussion of the genre as a whole see N. Habel, "The Form and Significance of the Call Narratives," *Zeitschrift für die Alttestamentliche Wissenschaft* 77 (1965) 297–323. Though the latter publication is German, the article by Habel does appear in English.

4. The concept of the holy as basis for all religious experience is examined in a classical study by R. Otto, *The Idea of the Holy* (London: Oxford University Press, 1958).

5. The relevant passages are as follows: Jer 12:1–5; 15:10–11, 15–21; 17:14–18; 18:18–23; and 20:7–18.

Chapter Three

"Fear Not":
Faith and Trust in the Bible

A crucial element of psychological and spiritual growth consists of learning to face up to the fears which tie us down and hold us back. Many psychologists as well as a considerable number of popular books on personal development see the task of dealing with fear as essentially a process of growing in trust. As we learn to be more trusting of God, of the life-process, and of ourselves, we become liberated from fear through an experience which is often described as a releasing, letting go, or surrender. It is very interesting to observe that this insight, popularized today in best-selling books and in widely attended workshops or seminars, is precisely the understanding which emerges from a study of the motif of faith or trust in the Old Testament.

Regarding the polarity between fear and trust, there is an immediate connection between the results of scholarship and the practical application in real life situations. This is in contrast, for example, to the material presented in Chapter One, where the experiential processes involved more of a creative and imaginative adaptation of the biblical material. As a result, it seems appropriate to try to convey a general idea of the kind of evidence and the type of reasoning involved in the critical investigation of this issue. Nonetheless, the following overview, which deals principally with philological matters, will probably be of more interest to some readers than to others.

Consequently, I wish to point out that the understanding of the experiential exercises in section 3 of the chapter does not depend upon a careful study of the more technical information presented in the first two sections.

1. Philological Considerations

It is a feature of Hebrew, the language in which the Old Testament was originally written, that a whole family of words can be formed by a series of variations on a basic root or stem. Most of these roots consist of three consonants, i.e., *gdl*. When the stem *gdl* occurs with the vocalization *gādal* we have the simple form of the verb meaning "to grow up, become great." By prefixing the letter *h* and changing the vocalization to *higdîl* we get the so-called hiphil form of the verb which means, "to make great or enlarge." The form *gādôl* is an adjective meaning, "great." On the other hand *godel* and *gĕdûlāh* are both abstract nouns meaning "greatness."

Of special interest to us is the way in which the various verbal forms are constructed. We have already mentioned that the simple form *gādal*, "to be great," can be transformed into a hiphil form *higdîl*, meaning "to make great." Another example is *zākar*, "to remember," which can be transformed to a hiphil form *hizqîr*, "to cause to remember, to remind." There is another form, called the niphal, which in this case produces *nizkar*, "to be remembered." For our purposes it is sufficient to know about these three modifications of the verbal stem (simple form, niphal and hiphil). There are other verbal forms which occur in the language, but they do not need to be considered here.

Note that in the case of the roots *gdl* and *zkr*, the transformation from the simple form to the hiphil expresses the causative aspect of the concept expressed in the simple form ("to be great" becomes "to make great"; "to remember" becomes "to remind"). Moreover, the niphal transformation for the root *zkr* expresses a passive concept ("to remember" becomes "to be remembered"). It happens very often in the language that the niphal represents the passive and the hiphil expresses a causative notion. This means that when one knows the meaning of the simple form of the verb, it is often possible to guess the meaning of the other two forms. However, there are many cases where the meaning of the niphal and hiphil can not be so easily predicted. Moreover, there are some roots for which the niphal and/or the hiphil are documented, but where the simple form does not exist in Biblical Hebrew.

With the above information as background, we are ready to move on to the subject matter of the chapter. The Hebrew verb which is usually translated "to believe" is *he'ĕmîn,* a hiphil form derived from the root *'mn.*[1] The same root occurs in the Hebrew word *'āmēn* which has been taken over into English as, "Amen," and which we all know as an expression used to conclude a prayer. How can we determine the precise meaning of the hiphil verb based on this stem *'mn*? The task is complicated by the fact that the Hebrew Bible does not contain any usage of the simple form of this verb. That is, either the simple form never existed, or it fell out of usage at some stage of the Hebrew language preceding the writing of the Old Testament.

How then can we, along with all the researchers who have studied this question before, figure out the precise meaning of *he'ĕmîn*?[2] There are three basic approaches which can be tried:

a. Basic Root Meaning. Sometimes it is possible to figure out a basic central meaning attached to a root. In the example given above of different variations on the root *gdl,* the concept of "greatness" was the basic underlying idea. If we could determine a basic underlying idea in the root *'mn*, that might help determine the precise significance of the hiphil verb.

b. Related Verbal Forms. Although there are no cases of the simple verb form of the root *'mn*, there is a significant number of examples of the niphal form of this verb. Studying the meaning of the niphal could help throw light on the meaning of the hiphil.

c. Examination of Context. If one looked up every passage in the Old Testament where the hiphil verb form of the root *'mn* occurred, it would be possible in many cases to figure out the meaning, or its nuances, from the context.

We will go ahead and see what results from these three lines of inquiry.

a. Basic Root Meaning. The conventional view found in standard dictionaries and many philological studies is that the basic meaning of the root *'mn* is "to be firm, sure, reliable." On this basis, it has been argued that the hiphil verb means "to consider someone or something as being firm, sure, or reliable," hence, "to trust, depend upon." Such an explanation of the meaning of *he'ĕmîn* is attractive to many people from a theological point of view. However, recent studies have pointed out that the determination of a basic root meaning must be founded upon an examination of what is meant by each of the derived forms of the stem. To then try to determine the meaning of the hiphil derivative on the basis of the proposed root meaning involves a circular argument. Moreover, some scholars today question the validity of attaching a meaning to the root itself in abstraction from the specific forms. Our first possible line of investigation, therefore, does not lead to dependable results.

b. Related Verbal Forms.   Since, as indicated above, the meaning of a hiphil verb form is often related to the meaning of the simple form, a study of the latter might seem to be recommended as a good starting point. Unfortunately, the simple verb form of the root *'mn* was not used in Biblical Hebrew.[3] Consequently we will begin by reviewing the use of *ne'ĕman*, the niphal form of the root, a form which does occur fairly often in contexts which make the meaning relatively easy to define.

The niphal apparently means, "to be constant, lasting, reliable." For example, the Hebrew *ne'ĕman* is used in Isa 33:1 for a dependable source of water, whereas in Jer 15:18 a brook which dries up is equivalent to water which is not *ne'ĕman*. In Isa 22:23, 25, a peg which is securely driven in so that it will not get pulled out is said to be in a *ne'ĕman* place.

The term can also be applied to persons. For example, in Prov 25:13 it refers to a messenger upon whom his master can rely. A passage in Ps 78:37 is particularly interesting. There it is said that the Israelites had not been *ne'ĕman* towards God. The statement is elaborated upon by saying that "they were not faithful to his covenant." This makes clear just what kind of constancy or reliability is meant by the word. Similarly, the term is used in reference to God in Isa 49:7 and Deut 7:9, meaning that he is "the God on whom one can rely, who keeps his promise."[4]

An especially important example is found in 2 Sam 7, a chapter which contains the dynastic promise reported to David by the prophet Nathan. The oracle points out that although God had originally chosen Saul to be king, that choice had been revoked. The choice of David is different, however, for it will last forever. This constancy is expressed in verse 16 by saying that David's house, or dynasty, will be *ne'ĕman*, that is to say, "permanent."

So for the niphal, we will be on solid ground if we agree with the following formulation:

If one were to try to find a translation in English that would embrace the different meanings of this word, the closest would probably be "constant," which can include both the permanency of things and the stability and reliability of persons. The result is that one may build or rely upon the thing or person giving proof of constancy.[5]

This meaning of the niphal form can be kept in the back of our minds as we go on to look at the hiphil form.

c. The Use of the Hiphil in Context.

The hiphil form of *'mn*, transcribed *he'ĕmîn*, occurs about 50 times in the Old Testament. Obviously, we can not examine all of them in this chapter, but it will be helpful to look at a few examples.

One of the most significant occurrences of *he'ĕmîn* is in Isa 7:9. To get at its meaning, it is necessary to look at the whole passage, Isa 7:1–9. The situation is that the northern Kingdom of Israel (capital: Samaria; king: Pekah the son of Remaliah) and the kingdom of the Syrians or Aramaeans (capital: Damascus; king: Rezin) are attempting to form a military coalition to stop the advancing might of the Assyrian Empire. When Ahaz, the current representative of the Davidic dynasty ruling over the Kingdom of Judah, refused to join this alliance, his capital city of Jerusalem was attacked by Pekah and Rezin. They intended to do away with Ahaz and replace him with a new king, not of the Davidic family, who would go along with the coalition. This was, therefore, a very grave crisis which threatened the very existence of the Davidic dynasty whose permanence had been promised according to the oracle of Nathan found in 2 Sam 7 and discussed above.

According to Isa 7:2, when the "house of David," that is, Ahaz, was informed about the siege, "his heart and the heart of his people trembled as the trees of the forest tremble in the wind." In other words, they were all terrified. Such fear is an indication that they did not have very much confidence in the promises made concerning the Davidic dynasty, for if they trusted those assurances, they would have realized that there was nothing to worry about. This is, in fact, the point of view presented by the prophet Isaiah who brought a message from God saying, "Take care, be quiet, and let your heart not be afraid." That is, an attitude of calm and serenity is the appropriate response to this situation, for God will certainly be true to His promises and defeat the enemies of the Davidic dynasty. However, as if sensing the king's inability to conform to this model, the prophet ended the message with a warning recorded in verse 9, "If you do not *he'ĕmîn* you will not be *ne'ĕman.*" There is a play on words here involving the hiphil and the niphal of the root *'mn.* Moreover, the use of the niphal form, as indeed other indications in the passage, were apparently intended by the author to remind us of the dynastic oracle in 2 Sam 7. The conditional statement in Isa 7:9 does not take back the promise of 2 Sam 7:16 that the dynasty will be *ne'ĕman,* but it does say that King Ahaz himself will not be *ne'ĕman,* "kept secure," unless he has the proper attitude, expressed by the hiphil form *he'ĕmîn.*

What then, precisely, is Ahaz being asked to do in the warning given in Isa 7:9 and what is meant there by *he'ĕmîn?* Apparently, it amounts to the same thing as the command issued in verse 4, "Take care, be quiet, and let not your heart be afraid." That is, it is an inner attitude of calm and serenity which arises from a sense of trust and confidence that God will be true to his promises. The same concept is expressed by Isaiah in different words at 30:15, "In returning and rest you will be saved; your strength is in quietness and trust." It is interesting to note that in 7:9 and 28:16 Isaiah uses the verb *he'ĕmîn* in an "absolute" sense, that is, without an object. In other words, the verb is intransitive in meaning (or internally transitive) and refers primarily to a phenomenon within the sub-

ject of the verb rather than the impact which that action might
have on an object outside of the speaker. In fact, it is characteristic of the hiphil of '*mn* that it does not take a direct object,
although in many cases (see below) it is complemented by a
prepositional phrase.

Another important passage for understanding *he'ĕmîn* is
Deut 1:26–33. Moses is reminding the people of that moment
in the period of wilderness wandering when God had issued
the command to go into the promised land, conquer it, and
take possession of it. Moses relates:

> But you did not want to attack. You rebelled against the
> command of your God and complained against your God
> saying, "It is because the Lord hates us that he has
> brought us out of Egypt, to hand us over to the Amorites
> so they can kill us. What kind of place are we supposed to
> be entering? Our compatriots have made our hearts melt
> when they said, 'There is a great people, taller than we
> and cities fortified as high as the sky, and we even saw
> giants there!' " At that time I answered you, "Do not be
> terrified of them and do not fear. It is the Lord your God
> who goes before you. He it is who will fight for you as
> everything he did with you in Egypt before your very
> eyes. And in the desert you saw how the Lord carried you
> just as a man carries his child, along the whole path which
> you travelled until you reached this place." But in spite of
> this speech, you did not *he'ĕmîn* in the Lord your God.

Just as in the Isaiah passage, whatever *he'ĕmîn* signifies it excludes the experiencing of fear. The issue is not whether they
"believe," in the usual English sense of that word. It is not a
matter of their believing in God, or believing what Moses said
in his speech, namely that it is God who carried them through
safely thus far. In fact, in the speech of the people they explicitly acknowledge that they believe this. The problem is

that they don't trust God's intentions. They do not doubt that it is God who has given the command to go ahead and invade, but they think God's purpose is to get them killed. The assertion strikes us as almost bizarre—surely a sign of a profound deterioration of a relationship where trust has given way to suspicion of malicious intent. It would appear, therefore, that the most satisfactory English equivalent for the hiphil form of *'mn* in the passage quoted above is "trust." Even at that, it does not hurt to point out that "God," which is preceded by the prepositional prefix *b* in Hebrew, is not the direct object of the verb. The emphasis is on the state or condition manifested within the subject of the verb. Were it not so awkward, one might suggest that the sense of the Hebrew would be more adequately conveyed by a translation such as, "you would not adopt an attitude of trust and confidence in relation to God."

Finally, let us look briefly at Gen 15:1–5. God appears to Abraham and tells him "Fear not." The patriarch, however, has something to be concerned about: he does not have a son to be his heir. God then takes him outside and says, "Count the stars if you can. . . . So shall your descendants be." Then Abraham did whatever is meant by *he'ĕmîn*. As in the other two texts, *he'ĕmîn* is parallel to not being afraid. It refers to a serene trust in God and in God's promise. Actually, in this case, the translation "believe" would express the meaning fairly well. However, it should be clear from the context that more is involved than merely giving intellectual assent to the truth of a factual statement.

Another interesting aspect of Abraham's act of trusting is that God "reckoned it to him as righteousness (RSV)." Here we have an important theological affirmation which was later taken up in the New Testament: that which "makes a person right with God" is precisely the confident, trusting attitude expressed by the hiphil of the verb *'mn*. The word therefore expresses a very important concept for understanding the theology of the Old Testament.

We have seen in the examples given above that *he'ĕmîn* is contrasted with fear. The juxtaposition of the two attitudes apparently goes back to the phenomenon of the "holy war" which prevailed especially in the time of the Judges. The idea was that the wars fought in those times were quite literally Yahweh's wars and that He was the one who won the victory. Any soldier who was afraid demonstrated by his fear that he did not have confidence in Yahweh's ability to win this battle. Consequently such a person was disqualified from participating in combat. The dismissal of fearful members of the army is reflected in Deut 20:8 and Judg 7:2–3. More specifically, the contrast between fear and trust *(he'ĕmîn)* in the context of warfare is also found in Num 14:9–11; 2 Chr 20:13–20 (compare especially verses 15 and 20); and Deut 28:66. Later in history, the prophets removed the "Fear not" exhortations from their original military context and used them for other purposes. Such was done with special effectiveness during the Babylonian captivity by Second Isaiah in passages which do not happen to use the word *he'ĕmîn* but still deserve study as a reflection of the trusting attitude we have been speaking of: Isa 40:9; 41:10,13,14; 43:1,5; 44:2; 51:7; 54:4 (see also 51:12 and 54:14).

Before ending our discussion of the meaning of the hiphil form of the verb *'mn*, it is necessary to acknowledge that there are some cases where it does in fact mean to believe in the truth of some message. For example, the Queen of Sheba says in 1 Kgs 10:7 that she did not believe the reports about Solomon's wisdom until she visited him and saw with her own eyes. Here, as is normally the case when *he'ĕmîn* has this meaning, the noun expressing what is believed does not stand as the direct object of the verb, but is rather introduced by the prepositional prefix *l*. So the semantic development seems to have begun with a meaning like "to become trusting in connection with . . . ," and thus "to believe. . . ." The thrust of the case I have been trying to build in this section, is not that *he'ĕmîn* should never be translated "to believe," but that the essential notion is the subject's state of trust and confidence, a condition which excludes the possibility of anxiety and fear. It is from this essential notion that other meanings developed. These conclusions are in harmony with the results of the investigation of the niphal form of the same root which, as noted above, expresses the notion of "constancy."

2. The New Testament

The antithesis between fear and trust is also an important theme in the New Testament, which was written in Greek. There the word for fear is *phobeomai* (compare the English "phobia") and the verb which corresponds to *he'ĕmîn* is *pisteuō*. From the latter are derived the nouns *pistos*, "one who believes, trusts," and *oligopistos*, "one lacking in faith or trust." An important passage which reflects these motifs is the story about walking on the water in Matt 14:22–33. When the disciples see Jesus walking on the water they are terrified. The verb *phobeomai* is used in verses 26 and 27. Peter begins to walk out onto the water towards Jesus. Then he becomes fearful *(phobeomai)* and begins to sink. Jesus says to him, "You person without trust *(oligopistos)*, why did you become fearful *(phobeomai)?*" As in the Old Testament, the fundamental attitude which is enjoined by this Gospel passage is a serene confidence which excludes the possibility of fear. The same trusting attitude is recommended in the often quoted passage Matt 10:29–31:

> Are not two sparrows sold for a penny? And not one of
> them will fall to the ground without your Father's will. But
> even the hairs of your head are all numbered. Fear not
> (*phobeomai*), therefore, you are of more value than many
> sparrows. (RSV).

There are yet other passages using the verb *phobeomai*
which reflect the same "Fear not" theme as is found in the Old
Testament. However, one of the most important and memo-
rable passages with this theme is Matt 6:25–34, part of the Ser-
mon on the Mount, which uses a different Greek verb,
merimnaō which means "to be anxious, worry." Those who
give in to anxious fear are said to be persons lacking in faith
(*oligopistos*):

> Therefore I tell you, do not be anxious about your life,
> what you shall eat or what you shall drink, nor about your
> body, what you shall put on. Is not life more than food,
> and the body more than clothing? Look at the birds of the
> air: they neither sow nor reap nor gather into barns, and
> yet your heavenly Father feeds them. Are you not of more
> value than they? And which of you by being anxious can
> add one cubit to his span of life? And why are you anxious
> about clothing? Consider the lilies of the field, how they
> grow; they neither toil nor spin; yet I tell you, even Sol-
> omon in all his glory was not arrayed like one of these. But
> if God so clothes the grass of the field, which today is alive
> and tomorrow is thrown into the oven, will he not much
> more clothe you, O men of little faith? Therefore do not
> be anxious, saying, "What shall we eat?" or "What shall
> we drink?" or "What shall we wear?" For the Gentiles
> seek all these things; and your heavenly Father knows that
> you need them all. But seek first his kingdom and his
> righteousness, and all these things shall be yours as well.
> Therefore, do not be anxious about tomorrow, for tomor-

row will be anxious for itself. Let the day's own trouble be
sufficient for the day. (RSV).

Still another word meaning "fearful" is the Greek *deilos*.
This is the word used in Matt 8:26 and Mark 4:40 in the story
of the calming of the storm. Jesus has fallen asleep in the boat
and a great storm arises at sea. The disciples are terrified and
awaken him. His reaction is, "Why are you afraid *(deilos)*, O
men of little faith *(oligopistos)?*" The message is precisely the
same as that found in the story of Peter walking on the water.

There is also a striking passage in Rev 21:8 where the person who is fearful *(deilos)* is linked with the unbeliever *(apis-
tos)*. And finally, there is a verb formed on the same root
(deiliaō), which occurs only once in the New Testament, but
in a moving passage which well summarizes what both testaments have to say on this subject. This is John 14:27:

> Peace I leave with you; my peace I give to you; . . . Let
> not your hearts be troubled, neither let them be afraid.
> (RSV).

3. Experiential Process

One of the occasions on which I have used this material
with a group was a workshop offered for one hour of graduate
credit in an M.A. program in Pastoral Ministries. The results
which are reported in this section come principally from that
experience, though I have also presented this workshop to
other groups.

The graduate mini-course met for four sessions of two
hours and fifteen minutes each. These class meetings were
about equally divided between a traditional academic format
and experiential process. The lectures presented the infor-

mation summarized above, though in considerably greater detail.

In the first experiential component, I proposed to the participants that if we wanted to appropriate for ourselves in a genuinely existential fashion what the Bible teaches about fear and trust, we would have to do something which is not usually done in a classroom—which, in fact, is not often done at all: we would have to take an honest look at our own fears. Unfortunately, many of us have layers of fears lying one over the other. We are afraid to admit to ourselves that we are afraid. And certainly, we are afraid of allowing other people to find out just how many fears we have.

When I ask of a group that they begin to break through these layers of fear, it is my practice to participate in the process along with them, modelling the self-disclosure which I am suggesting. My preparation for this led to an interesting learning experience. One evening, I jotted down as many of my own fears as I could think of. I then typed out the list under the heading, "Some of Conrad's fears:" and slipped the page into a notebook. There were almost 40 items on the list including such things as fear of dying, that there might be something wrong with me, that people won't like me, that I'll end up looking foolish, etc. The list included some points I was not sure I was ready to share with others yet.

Next day, I threw the notebook onto the seat of my car while driving my twelve year old son to school. After a few minutes, I noticed that he had picked up my list and had read it. I gulped and frantically tried to remember what might be on that list that I did not want him to read. My fears seem confirmed when he asked, "Wow, Dad, are you really afraid of all these things?" I hesitantly answered, "Yes. Don't you have some things that you are afraid of?" His response taught me something important. He said, "Oh sure. I'm afraid of most of the things you have here and lots more besides. I just didn't think you adults had fears like this too." I realized that by trying to protect our children we sometimes create in them the impression that they are alone in their fears. No wonder they grow up thinking it is not OK to let other people know what's going on inside them!

When it came to sharing some of my fears with the class, I read some of the items from my list. More important, however, I wanted to be open about fears which I was in touch with at that very moment. I admitted that I had fears that this particular mini-course would not work out as I wanted it to. I told them that this was especially scary because I was trying to move out into what was a new direction for me and that if this course was not "successful" it might mean that the dream I had about developing new techniques and approaches might seem to be impossible to achieve. I also admitted that I knew some of them had signed up for this course because they had taken another course from me and had liked it, but I experienced the fear that this time I might not live up to those expectations and they would be disappointed. So I shared as well as I could what were my actual here-and-now feelings.

I then gave the students a chance to share some of their fears, pointing out that it would be easier if they began with fears which they had experienced in the past and more difficult (though more helpful) if they dealt with here-and-now fears. As can be expected in a diverse group, some were more cautious and stuck to safer material while others took greater risks. One student, who had arrived quite late for class, reported his fears about how I and the rest of the class would react to his lateness. He told of how, when he first looked into the room and saw people sitting around in a circle and interacting in ways that did not correspond to his expectations of what a graduate class would be, he worried about what he was getting into. These fears seemed to be dissipated as a result of being verbalized and his sharing promoted a feeling of closeness between him and the rest of the class.

As an additional assignment, I asked the participants to keep a journal for the next few days and to record whatever fears they became aware of. I suggested that any time they were emotionally upset or in any way unhappy, they might ask themselves questions such as "What am I afraid is going to happen? What is it that I want and am afraid I won't get? What am I afraid I will lose?"

On the next class day, I asked them to discuss what they had learned about themselves by doing journal work on their fears. They had all done a very serious job of this. One of the women in the class gave a moving account of the struggle she had gone through in trying to share more of her genuine self with other persons; how afraid she was of opening herself to other people lest she be hurt; how a number of experiences in which she felt that others had betrayed her trust had hurt her so much that now she even feared trusting God because He might let her down too. Her words came out haltingly at times through the intensity of her emotion and she wept. The quality of the listening and accepting from the others was almost tangible as we all experienced the compassion, the oneness and the love which become possible when one human being risks letting herself be herself in the presence of others. In spite of her fears, she showed that she had begun to trust us and we were grateful for the gift she was giving to us.

This period of sharing was followed by a meditation or a guided imagery process. I pointed out before starting that in this process I would refer to the "Wise Teacher." They could take this as a reference to Jesus or to any other person, past, present, or even imaginary, whom they viewed as the embodiment of wisdom and love. We used systematic bodily relaxation as a lead into the meditation proper. Then I guided them with the following instructions:

> Close your eyes and visualize some place where you enjoy walking by yourself. It might be a real garden or wooded area which has special significance for you personally, or a place which you create within your imagination. Imagine yourself walking in this place, reflecting on the work you have just been doing with your fears. Be aware of the parts of that which you have shared in the group as well as parts which had perhaps been too hard to share. As you are slowly and thoughtfully strolling along, you become aware of someone up ahead who seems to be waiting. As you get closer, you realize that it is the Wise Teacher who has been waiting there just for you. You can see that the Wise Teacher is perfectly delighted that you are the one who has come along at this time for he (or she) has been waiting just for you. The Wise Teacher knows that you have shared a lot about your fears and that there is a lot more that you want to share and that he (or she) is there to listen. So in the awareness that the Wise Teacher understands completely, you spend a few minutes sharing those parts of your fears which you can share with nobody else.

After 2 or 3 minutes of silence, I continued as follows:

> The Wise Teacher now asks for a gift from you saying, "I want you to choose a fear which you especially want to be free of and give it to me as a present." With your eyes still closed, hold your hands out in front of you, palms up, and visualize the fear you are working with in your hands. Let whatever visual symbol for that fear which may arise just come into your imagination. The Wise Teacher's hands are extended too. Very slowly, reach out and place that fear in the hands of the Wise Teacher. As it leaves your

hands and enters the hands of the Wise Teacher, you are surprised to see your fear start to change. It begins to radiate a bright golden light which becomes more and more intense until your fear has been transformed into something of great beauty. The Wise Teacher thanks you for this gift and turns to leave, reminding you that the two of you can meet again at this same place at another time.

I then instructed them to gradually bring themselves back to the reality of the room we were in. We spent a few minutes discussing how they had experienced this exercise.

Whenever I lead a group in this visualization/meditation, a number of reactions typically occur. There is frequently a realization of how deeply participants want to unburden themselves of the fears they have locked up within. A profound sense of release and freedom is experienced when they recognize that Jesus, or another Wise Teacher, has enough love and acceptance and understanding that they are able to share their inmost fears in the visualization. The concept that a fear could just be given away is a novel idea for many people. They sometimes find, however, that in the imagery process they were actually able to let go of something they had been holding onto for a long time. Moreover, they have an experience of what it feels like to give over a fear and having done it once, they know experientially how to do it again. Finally, there is the realization that to someone with great love and great wisdom, the terrible secret you were trying to hide can be a thing of great beauty. This aspect of the meditation process is often experienced as surprising and unexpected. The new perspective can have a powerful healing effect as a person discovers a way to be more accepting of a part of the self which had previously been rejected.

Sometimes a participant will say, "I could visualize a particular fear very clearly, but I just could not let go of it. It stayed right in my own hands." I believe it is important to re-assure such persons that whatever happened for them in the process is perfectly OK and is an opportunity for them to learn something which can be helpful for them. In this particular case, I would ask these persons to close their eyes again and visualize the scene in which they are trying to give the fear to the Wise Teacher but can not let go of it. Then I suggest that they ask the Wise Teacher whatever questions they might have, such as "Why can't I let go of it?" I also tell them to ob-serve how the Wise Teacher is reacting to the fact that they can not let go of the fear. Most persons who do this experience an answer such as "You're not quite ready to let go of it yet, but you will be soon," or, "You still need it for now." And in-variably, their experience is that the Wise Teacher is com-pletely accepting of their inability to let go. As a facilitator in such a process, I don't have to worry about what might happen or try to figure out beforehand how I will answer any questions which may arise. The process itself can be trusted. Or rather, the inner wisdom of the individual participants, which is ac-cessed through the imagery, can be trusted to have the an-swers which they need.

During the next class meeting of the mini-course, we used a bodily exercise to explore the phenomenon of trust. One at a time, a student would sit on a bench in such a way that when he or she leaned back into a horizontal position the lower part of the back would be supported by the bench but the rest of the torso and the head were supported only by the hands of three or four other group members. The person doing the exercise was told just to experience what it is like to trust. With eyes closed, this person would very slowly begin to lean back until he or she felt the hands of the others supporting the head and body. The truster had to be reminded to breathe—breathe deeply and let go more and more. Finally, the per-son's upper body was parallel to the floor and completely supported by the hands of others. I suggested, "Just see what it's like to trust, to put yourself in someone else's hands." Once the truster had relaxed sufficiently, we gently rocked the body back and forth and chanted to him or her. One of the chants used was the following:

> Listen, listen, listen to my heart's song.
> Listen, listen, listen to my heart's song.
> I will never forget you, I will never forsake you.
> I will never forget you, I will never forsake you.[6]

For some of the participants we used this other chant:

> I love you as you are, my child,
> Let go your every fear.
> Look within and you will find,
> That I am always here.[7]

In the sharing which took place afterwards, several remarked that the hardest part was when they first began to lean back, when they did not as yet feel the supporting hands beneath them but had to let themselves go back anyway. Some reported that even when the weight was totally supported by the other participants they had to make an effort to keep letting go. As they did so, some experienced a feeling of lightness or euphoria.

One of the main ideas behind this activity is that letting go and trusting are behaviors which we can get better at through practice. By observing how we have experienced the letting go in an exercise which uses the body, we become familiar with our own peculiar way of doing this. Next time we feel our fears overtaking us, we can remember how we let go once before and do it again. Such a method of learning engages our emotional and bodily experience along with the intellectual understanding.

On the last day of class, we all participated in a discussion of how the biblical teaching on trust and fear related to our own personal journeys. There was a consensus that when we trust God absolutely, we may not get what it was that we thought we wanted, but that we change so profoundly that what we do have in our lives is seen in a different light as the perfect expression of God's gracious love for us.

We spent some time discussing practical steps we could take so that what we had been learning could continue to work in our lives. We could, for example, continue to use a journal to become aware of how fear operates in our lives. There might be a danger here of becoming judgmental about ourselves and feeling disappointed as we notice that we are still holding on to many fears. So a first step would be to love and accept ourselves even when we notice these fears coming up. An aid to doing this could be the chant "I love you as you are," which was quoted previously. The next step which might be taken is to find someone who is a good listener and share it with that person. For we had found in our group that sometimes a specific fear was greatly deflated just by being talked about.

Some other possibilities for journal work would be to try to see if we were getting some kind of payoff from the fear. Perhaps, for example, being afraid of not doing a good job gives me the feeling that I am a reliable and responsible person. Or there might be, under our fear, some limiting belief which we could examine. For example, the fear of offending someone by stating clearly what we think is based on the belief that we are responsible for other people's feelings. That is a belief we might consider changing. In short, there are a number of simply psychological changes which could help us to more effectively get what we want out of life without using fear to motivate or limit us.

More immediately concerned with spirituality would be the practice of turning our fears over into the hands of God.

This could involve a simple prayer like, "God, take this fear away from me," or "Lord, I am now ready to stop holding onto this fear." We could remember the visualization process with the Wise Teacher and once again "give" our fear to God or the Wise Teacher. Another helpful practice is to memorize one of the "Fear not" passages from Second Isaiah. For example, Isa 41:13:

> For I, the Lord your God,
>   hold your right hand;
> it is I who say to you, "Fear not,
>   I will help you." (RSV).

In those passages which name Jacob or Israel, we can substitute our own names, as in Isa 44:2:

> Thus says the Lord who made you,
>   who formed you from the womb and will help you:
> "Fear not, O _____my servant,
>   _____ whom I have chosen. (RSV).

Similarly effective in this regard are songs like Bob Dufford's "Be Not Afraid,"[8] or Psalms such as 23 and 131.

There are also some practices which could help us grow in the attitude of trust. One would be to keep reminding ourselves of the exercise in which we leaned back until our upper bodies were supported by the hands of others. Our bodies will remember how we did this and can help us to "let go" in other circumstances. Or we could just lie on our backs on the floor and allow ourselves to become fully aware of how the floor is supporting us, how we can sink freely and completely into the floor and it holds us up without our needing to do anything at all. We can use this to remind ourselves of the way in which we are supported by God.

Growing in trust also involves a willingness to develop new attitudes towards ourselves, others, God and the world. We need to grow in love and acceptance of ourselves based on the conviction of our fundamental goodness as God's creatures, trusting the inner guidance which comes to us in the "still small voice" speaking in our hearts. As far as other persons are concerned, it is not so much a matter of naively entrusting them with our reputations, our material goods, or our physical well-being, but rather of trusting that they can be responsible for their own lives and that in fact they are doing the best they can with their lives on the basis of what they know and believe. Our primary task, then, is to forgive them when we think they have offended us, imitating the behavior of Jesus on the cross who said of his persecutors, "Father, forgive them, they know not what they do." Finally, our learning to trust God means to grow in the understanding that the world we live in is of God's making, not of our own. It is as God wants it to be. When we fully accept this truth here and now, there can be nothing to fear.

As we talked about practical ways of applying what we had learned and became aware of its many ramifications it became obvious that a whole spirituality could be developed on the basis of the biblical understanding of faith and trust. The time allotted for our being together was coming to an end, however. So I concluded the workshop with a visualization in which I asked the students to let their creativity operate with complete freedom to imagine what would become of them if they completely gave up their fears. We shared these personal dreams with one another and encouraged one another to believe that these dreams would indeed become a reality as we learned to let go and trust more and more in God, in the universe, in one another, and in ourselves.

Let me conclude my summary of this course by quoting an unedited self-report written by one of the participants.

Academically, I gained a greater understanding of and appreciation for the OT dialectic of fear/trust. This makes any study of Scripture richer. I also learned something about the way Jesus approached fear in the lives of the people around him. Finally, I again saw how important the nuances of language can be in understanding Scripture. A loosely paraphrased translation just doesn't do the job. It is important to be faithful to the different connotations of the various forms of words in order to understand their meaning. And, of course, equally important is some understanding of the historical context from which these ideas came. That was provided in the handouts and the mini-lectures.

Personally, while I didn't make any huge leaps in growth in the past two weeks, a couple of important things happened. (1) I recognized my own resistance to change, even in the areas where I think I want to change. For example, intellectually, I know that I don't like to be afraid. At the same time, I find myself afraid to let go of some of my fears. It's risky business to let go of the familiar, no matter how unpleasant it might be. (2) Some things that I knew, or suspected, were confirmed, and that is always a good experience. I know that I am the one who is in control of how I feel, but it is so easy for me to let that knowledge slip into the background, just beyond my conscious awareness. The practical ideas you offered for dealing with fear reminded me once more that the way I feel really is my choice. (3) One very rewarding part of the class was the interaction with the other students. It also felt good to let them know something about me. I felt closer to them as a result. I learned (for the hundredth time) that we all really do have the same fears and doubts. Hearing that in what they said gave me so much more empathy for each of them. I want to work on remembering that and applying empathy even when I don't know the particular fears of a given individual.

NOTES

1. The symbol ' stands for the Hebrew letter alef which represents a consonantal sound called a "glottal stop" which is produced by closing off the throat with the back of the tongue. Since we do not have a corresponding letter in our alphabet, we more or less arbitrarily choose a symbol to represent it. The other two letters in '*mn* are named mem and nun in Hebrew. Since the three consonants can't be pronounced without vowels, scholars often use the pronunciation '*āman* to refer to this root.

2. For fuller discussion, see the following: A. Weiser, "The stem '*mn* and Related Expressions," in *Theological Dictionary of the New Testament*, trans. G. W. Bromiley (Grand Rapids: Eerdmans, 1968) Vol. 6, pp. 183–196; A. Jepsen, " '*āman*," in *Theological Dictionary of the Old Testament*, ed. G. J. Botterweck and H. Ringren (Grand Rapids: Eerdmans, 1977) Vol. 1, pp. 292–323; J. Barr, *The Semantics of Biblical Language* (Oxford: Oxford University Press, 1961) pp. 161–187; H. Wildberger, " '*mn* fest, sicher," *Theologisches Handwörterbuch zum Alten Testament*, ed. E. Jenni and C. Westermann (Munich: Chr. Kaiser Verlag, 1971) Vol. 1, cols. 177–209.

3. Actually, there is a word which occurs as '*ōmen* in the masculine and '*ōmenet* in the feminine and which some scholars take to be a participle of the simple form of the verb we are discussing. This word refers to reliable guardians who are entrusted with the care of dependent children. If we had solid grounds for associating the meaning of this participle with the meaning of the hiphil verb form, one might suggest that when the latter is related to God, it means to take towards God the same attitude that a child has towards an '*ōmen*. However attractive such a concept may be theologically, it can not claim solid philological support.

4. Jepsen, p. 295.

5. Jepsen, p. 298.

6. This chant was composed by Parmahansa Yogananda, founder of the Self-Realization Fellowship. It is quoted here from a cassette tape entitled *On Wings of Song "Many Blessings"* which is available from Spring Hill Music, Box 124, Ashby, MA 01431.

7. This is the refrain of a song by Robbie Gass entitled "As a Child." It is included on the cassette *Trust in Love* which is available from Spring Hill Music, Box 124, Ashby, MA 01431.

8. Published in *Glory and Praise: Songs for Christian Assembly* (Phoenix: North American Liturgy Resources, 1977).

Chapter Four

Dis-ease and Healing
in the Psalms

Critical scholarship has provided significant help for understanding the Psalms by clarifying the characteristic styles of prayer which are found in the Old Testament.[1] There are two principal modes which serve as the poles between which prayer moves back and forth. First, in a situation of need, one turns to God in *lament*. Then, in the awareness of the benefits received from God, including divine help in a specific situation of need, one proceeds to express *praise*.

The use of lament in the ancient world, including the Old Testament, reflects a cultural and psychological perspective which differs from what we modern Westerners are used to. In our culture, a person experiencing the need for divine help turns to God primarily with a prayer of petition in which one quite simply asks God for whatever help it is he or she is seeking. The ancient peoples also had such petitions in their prayers, but they placed much more emphasis on the description of the situation of need. This description, sometimes carried on at great length, is intended to awaken the pity of the god or goddess addressed in prayer. The more desperate the situation appears, the greater the likelihood that the deity will be motivated to help. This kind of "complaining," found so pervasively in the Book of Lamentations, for example, is what is meant by the term "lament."

At the other pole of devotional life is the prayer of praise which enters in after one has experienced the help sought for in the lament. In our culture, the usual response would be to give thanks. Here again, however, the ancient cultures had a different emphasis. Their response was to proclaim in public what had happened and to invite others to join in the praise of the god or goddess who had intervened in a time of need. Such praise shares the spontaneous psychological dynamism of the child's exclamation, "Grandma, you make the best chocolate chip cookies in the world!" or the boast, "My bike was broken, but my Daddy fixed it for me. He's a wonderful Daddy!" The immediacy and naturalness of praise contrasts with the artificiality of saying "Thank you," a mere social convention in which children need to be indoctrinated in order to conform.

Focusing now on the lament, we turn our attention to a specific category or genre called the lament of the individual. There are many examples of this particular genre in the Book of Psalms. These are the prayers of persons who came to the temple to present their needs to God in time of sickness, attack by enemies, or other life crises. It is possible to analyze these psalms in terms of a number of typical component parts which are usually easy to identify. First there is the invocation of God. This might simply consist of "O Lord," or it might be expanded into a more elaborate address to God. Then comes the lament proper, that is, the complaining about the distress experienced by the person who is saying the prayer. Frequently, the complaint has three aspects to it: (1) the physical and emotional pain felt by the individual; (2) the hostile attitude of other people, be they enemies or alleged friends; (3) even the behavior of God, who has failed to intervene as might have been expected. The third element in particular, reproaching God for not having acted, expresses a boldness in addressing God which seems disrespectful compared to our more deferential forms of prayer. In any case, the lament is followed by a petition, usually brief, which asks God to hear the prayer and to intervene. Next come expressions of trust—confidence that the prayer will in fact be answered. Then there is a vow of praise in which the person promises that after the requested help has been received, the lament will be followed up by the ritual of praise, thus completing the process moving between the two poles of prayer. Sometimes a psalm of this genre already begins the expression of praise, as if the prayer had already been answered. We can designate this phenomenon "anticipatory" praise. The various components of the lament of the individual, then, can be summarized as follows:

1. Invocation or address to God

2. Lament or complaint (refers to self, to enemies, and to God)

3. Petition for help

4. Trust or confidence

5. Vow of praise

6. Anticipatory praise

These six components typify the lament of the individual, although not every example of the genre contains all six components. Moreover, there are a few other parts which are only occasionally found and so have been omitted here for the sake of simplicity.

Sickness in the Laments of the Individual

In some of the laments of the individual, it is quite clear that the situation of need involves sickness. There are other cases, however, where it is difficult to be certain because the poetic language is open to various interpretations. The psalms which most clearly refer to sickness are Psalms 6, 22, 38, 39, 69, 88 and 102. Other related psalms which may perhaps belong here are 13, 28, 31, 35, 41, 70, and 109.

As we study the parts of these psalms which contain the lament or complaint, we cannot help but be impressed by the fact that they never treat physical illness as an isolated phenomenon. Quite to the contrary, these psalms present a multifaceted understanding of disease which includes physical, emotional, spiritual and social dimensions. Since the inclusive perspective found in the psalms is in agreement with current developments in the field of health care which increasingly sees healing and wellness in a holistic perspective, it will be valuable to give it a closer look.

First we have some examples of quotations from the Psalms reflecting the physical or bodily aspect of disease:

> I am like water poured out;
>   all my bones are racked.
> My heart has become like wax
>   melting away within my bosom.
> My throat is dried up like baked clay,
>   my tongue cleaves to my jaws;
>   to the dust of death you have brought me down.
> (Ps 22:15–16, NAB)

> Noisome and festering are my sores
>   because of my folly,
> I am stooped and bowed down profoundly;
>   all the day I go in mourning,
> For my loins are filled with burning pains;
>   there is no health in my flesh.
> (Ps 38:6–8, NAB)

> For my days vanish like smoke,
>   and my bones burn like fire.

Withered and dried up like grass is my heart;
    I forget to eat my bread.
Because of my insistent sighing
    I am reduced to skin and bone.
(Ps 102:4–6, NAB)

The element of emotional suffering is also very prominent in these psalms. Of course the connection of the feelings with physical pain is very close and already the passages quoted above hint at an emotional aspect. Some other quotations will bring this out even more clearly:

Have pity on me, O LORD, for I am in distress;
    with sorrow my eye is consumed;
        my soul also, and my body.
For my life is spent with grief
    and my years with sighing;
My strength has failed through affliction,
    and my bones are consumed.
(Ps 31:10–11, NAB)

For my soul is surfeited with troubles
    and my life draws near to the nether world.
I am numbered with those who go down into the pit;
    I am a man without strength.
My couch is among the dead,
    like the slain who lie in the grave,
Whom you remember no longer
    and who are cut off from your care.
You have plunged me into the bottom of the pit,
    into the dark abyss.
(Ps 88:4–7, NAB)

I am sunk in the abysmal swamp
    where there is no foothold;
I have reached the watery depths;

the flood overwhelms me.
I am wearied with calling,
    my throat is parched;
My eyes have failed with looking for my God.
(Ps 69:3–4, NAB)

The psalms dealing with sickness, then, portray very clearly and dramatically the inner situation of the sick person who not only has physical pain but deep emotional turmoil as well. So far, none of this is unexpected. But now we come to the social dimension which is not always recognized in our contemporary approach to questions of health. First, there are passages which speak of how the sick person's friends have turned away at the time of greatest need:

My friends and my companions stand back because of my
        affliction;
    my neighbors stand afar off.
(Ps 38:12, NAB)

Even my friend who had my trust
    and partook of my bread, has raised his heel against me.
(Ps 41:10, NAB)

You have taken my friends away from me;
    you have made me an abomination to them;
    I am imprisoned, and I cannot escape.
Companion and neighbor you have taken away from me;
    my only friend is darkness.
(Ps 88:9, 19, NAB)

But I, when they were ill, put on sackcloth;
    I afflicted myself with fasting
    and poured forth prayers within my bosom.
As though it were a friend of mine, or a brother, I went
        about;

> like one bewailing a mother, I was bowed down in
>   mourning.
> Yet when I stumbled they were glad and gathered together;
>   they gathered together striking me unawares.
> They tore at me without ceasing;
>   they put me to the test; they mocked me,
>   gnashing their teeth at me.
> (Ps 35:13–16, NAB)

The feeling expressed by the sick person of having been abandoned by friends in a time of need is one that modern readers
will be able to understand. Often, however, the laments of the
individual go even further than this, speaking of enemies who
seek to attack and kill the person:

> I hear the whispers of the crowd, that frighten me from every
>   side,
>   as they consult together against me, plotting to take my
>   life.
> (Ps 31:14, NAB)

> Many bullocks surround me;
>   the strong bulls of Bashan encircle me.
> They open their mouths against me
>   like ravening and roaring lions.
> (Ps 22:13–14, NAB)

> My enemies say the worst of me:
>   'When will he die and his name perish?'
> (Ps 41:6, NAB)

We will have more to say about these enemies later on.

The laments also reflect in a powerful manner the spiritual dimension of disease. The fundamental idea encountered
in this connection is that the sick person feels cut off from God
and abandoned:

> How long, O LORD? Will you utterly forget me?
>> How long will you hide your face from me?
> (Ps 13:2, NAB)

> My God, my God, why have you forsaken me,
>> far from my prayer, from the words of my cry?
> O my God, I cry out by day, and you answer not;
>> by night, and there is no relief for me.
> (Ps 22:2–3, NAB)

This alienation from God which results in the person's feeling spiritually isolated and alone is frequently linked with God's anger and the person's guilt:

> O LORD, in your anger punish me not,
>> in your wrath chastise me not;
> For your arrows have sunk deep in me,
>> and your hand has come down upon me.
> There is no health in my flesh because of your indignation;
>> there is no wholeness in my bones because of my sin,
> For my iniquities have overwhelmed me;
>> they are like a heavy burden, beyond my strength.
> (Ps 38:2–5, NAB)

Sometimes these thoughts are pushed so far that God almost appears to be an enemy who is attacking the person without reason:

> I was speechless and opened not my mouth,
>> because it was your doing;
> Take away your scourge from me;
>> at the blow of your hand I wasted away.
> With rebukes for guilt you chasten man;
>> you dissolve like a cobweb all that is dear to him;
>> only a breath is any man.
> Turn your gaze from me, that I may find respite

ere I depart and be no more.
(Ps 39:10–12, 14, NAB)

Why, O LORD, do you reject me;
    why hide from me your face?
I am afflicted and in agony from my youth;
    I am dazed with the burden of your dread.
Your furies have swept over me;
    your terrors have cut me off.
They encompass me like water all the day;
    on all sides they close in upon me.
(Ps 88:15–18, NAB)

The excerpts from the Psalms quoted above will clearly illustrate that in the biblical view, sickness involves physical, emotional, social and spiritual aspects. Individual psalms, of course, often emphasize one or the other dimension. Perhaps the best example of how all four dimensions are interwoven is found in Psalm 38. The reader is invited to go over that psalm in its entirety. It will be easy, on the basis of what has been said above, to pick out the verses which complain about each of the four aspects and thus become aware of how truly "holistic" is the Old Testament understanding of sickness and health.

Experiencing Our Dis-ease

The information from the psalms summarized above lends itself especially well to group work. It inevitably happens that many participants begin to experience healing through the very process of sharing with other persons in a small group. There is no need, then, to try to prove by logical argument that there is a social dimension to healing, because that fact is directly experienced and thus "learned" in the most effective way possible.

My assumption in structuring group exercises concerning this material is that we get to understand healing by becoming more fully aware of experiences of healing which we ourselves have gone through. Furthermore, accessing these experiences requires a willingness to get in touch with our need for healing. From the holistic perspective of the Psalms, this means awareness of bodily pain and disfunctions, emotional hurt, disruption and conflict in relationships, and spiritual alienation. All of this can be symbolized by the term "dis-ease" where the departure from normal spelling reminds us to think of the word as referring to a lack of harmony or wholeness in any aspect of our lives.

Much of the time, we exert a great deal of energy in concealing our dis-ease from ourselves and from others. Many of our social conventions are designed to maintain a facade of wellness which will prevent others from knowing what is really happening inside of us. This makes it even harder to admit to ourselves that we do not have an inner conviction of wholeness. If other people all have their lives together and are just perfectly happy, then it would mean that there is something terribly wrong with me if I acknowledged that much of the time what I experience is pain, turmoil and conflict. Such thoughts lead us into denial of our dis-ease. We don't want to look at it because we are afraid it will overwhelm us. We won't be able to handle it! In short, we are afraid of what we will find if we allow ourselves to become fully aware of our dis-ease.

It is because of the presence of such fears that, in my workshops on this topic, I begin with healing before working directly with dis-ease. To this end, I start by leading the group into a relaxed meditative state. Then I ask them to remember an occasion in the past on which they experienced some kind of healing. This might have been the mending of a broken bone, recovery from surgery, or the curing of some disease. The example need not involve traumatic pain or injury—the healing of a relatively harmless cut or even recovery from a common cold will serve the purpose. I tell participants to focus especially on the healing. Some of them might be able to access those memories in a visual manner, others would have a felt body-sense or kinesthetic memory of it, while others would have to "think" about it. In any case, I allow a couple minutes of silence for them to establish contact with what healing was for them in that situation. Then I ask "Exactly what is the process of healing for you? Where does the power for healing come from?" After a few more minutes of silence I say, "Now turn your attention to the part of your body in which you experienced that healing, or the part of your body that you associate with that healing. If you can easily put your hand on that part of your body, do so. Make a decision right now that this part of your body will from now on be a symbol to you that you have experienced healing in your life. (This is especially effective if there is some kind of scar remaining.) In the future, as you become aware of further need for healing, especially if you feel discouraged or overwhelmed, you can touch or remember this part of your body as a token of the fact that you do have access to healing power.

After this visualization, I divide the participants into groups of four or five in which they each have a couple of minutes to share with the others however much of that process which they care to verbalize. I make it quite clear that it is perfectly acceptable to keep to themselves whatever details they consider private. In this process of sharing, many individuals will observe that healing is a process which the bodily organism does for itself as long as the proper environment is maintained and the more or less automatic process is not interfered with. That is to say, without any suggestion from the group leader, the experience of participants will naturally lead many of them to become aware of their own inner healing power. Some will describe this as a power coming from God and made available through prayer. At the same time, the inner and spiritual aspects of healing do not necessarily exclude the help provided by health care professionals and the various technologies which they employ.

Having established an anchor or a grounding which will allow them to reconnect with a healing power, participants may feel safe enough to allow themselves to explore the dimension of dis-ease in their lives. I believe that if, as group leader, I am encouraging persons to expose their vulnerability, I should be willing to do the same. I therefore take ten to twenty minutes talking about the areas in my own life where I have experienced the deepest sense of dis-ease and the ways in which I have at least begun to move towards wholeness. I find that if I take the risk of self-disclosure, other group members begin to trust that it is safe to share a little more of themselves. Sometimes there will be one or two other people in the group whose stories I am familiar with and whom I can invite beforehand to be prepared to share their experience. All of this sets the atmosphere for the next steps.

The same small groups which worked together before sit in a square or circle. I ask them to decide who will go first. That individual turns to the person on his left and completes the sentence, "One of the areas of my life in which I experience dis-ease is. . . ." The person to whom the statement was made simply says, "Thank you for sharing that with me," then turns to his or her left and continues the process. The idea is to keep the statements brief and to go around the circle several times. Comments will include such items as "my relationship with my sister; a nagging pain in my lower back; my inability to complete my dissertation; a constant feeling that I am a failure; etc." After a while, I ask them to stop, remain silent for a few moments, and just look at the other persons in the small group and to become aware of what they are feeling about those persons and how they are feeling about themselves right at this moment. If time allows, I ask for a few persons to comment to the whole group about what the process has been like for them so far.

The completion of the sentence in the small group is meant as a gentle introduction into an exercise which might involve a greater intensity of feeling. With eyes closed, we return to a centered, meditative attitude. I then say something like the following:

> In the process which we are beginning, I am going to suggest that you allow an image to come to you. Don't try to think of what it should be and don't try to figure it out. Just be open to whatever comes. You can think of this as coming from your subconscious mind or from your creative imagination. Or you may think of it as in some way brought to you by the Spirit of God acting within you. So now just allow an image to come up—an image which symbolizes your dis-ease. You don't have to understand it. It may be visual, kinesthetic or auditory. Just become aware of it. (Pause) I am now going to instruct you to ask a question. Just trust that an answer will come and be open to whatever that answer is. Ask your image, "What is your name?" (Pause) Now ask your image, "What are you here to tell me?" (Pause) It is almost time for you to let this image go and come back into the awareness of this room which we are in. Before doing so, see if there is anything you need to do in order to complete the process with this image. You may have some other questions you want to ask. (Pause) Now say goodbye to this image and observe it separating itself from you and going away. Then, when you are ready, take a deep breath and as you release it, open your eyes and return to the reality of this room.

It is then a good idea to spend a few minutes allowing people to share as much of this visualization process as they want to in the small groups. If the group is going to disband for the time being and come back together on another occasion, I like to give them some optional "homework" assignments to do. One would be to do a drawing or a clay sculpture of the image of one's dis-ease as that came up in the visualization process. Afterwards a person could record what he or she felt about that image in a journal or private notebook. Another journal exercise is a dialogue between one's self and the image. One writes his or her own name on the left hand side of the page, followed by a colon, then the statement or question addressed to the image. Then the image's name is written at the beginning of a new line and the response is allowed to come up spontaneously and intuitively. The dialogue is continued until it comes to some kind of conclusion.

Whether or not individuals pursue such optional assignments, I strongly suggest that they read through once again the laments of the individual which deal with sickness (see above, p. 110) and identify some verses which, in the light of the experiential work done in the group, seem to fit their own situation in a particularly close way.

The Problem of Guilt

An important issue which arises in the laments of the individual is the problem of guilt. In some of these psalms, to begin with, we find that sickness is explicitly linked to sin and guilt:

> There is no health in my flesh because of your indignation;
> there is no wholeness in my bones because of my sin,
> For my iniquities have overwhelmed me;
> they are like a heavy burden, beyond my strength.
> (Ps 38:4–5, NAB)

The feeling of guilt and the corresponding need of forgiveness are expressed in an especially powerful manner in a group of psalms traditionally known as the Penitential Psalms, i.e. Pss 6, 32, 38, 51, 102, 130, 143. Of this category, Psalm 51 is particularly worth quoting even though it is not usually numbered among the psalms of the sick:

> For I know my transgressions,
>   and my sin is always before me.
> Against you, you only, have I sinned
>   and done what is evil in your sight,
> so that you are proved right when you speak
>   and justified when you judge.
> Surely I have been a sinner from birth,
>   sinful from the time my mother conceived me.
> Surely you desire truth in the inner parts;
>   you teach me wisdom in the inmost place.
> Cleanse me with hyssop, and I will be clean;
>   wash me, and I will be whiter than snow.
> Let me hear joy and gladness;
>   let the bones you have crushed rejoice.
> Hide your face from my sins
>   and blot out all my iniquity.
> Create in me a pure heart, O God,
>   and renew a steadfast spirit within me.
> Do not cast me from your presence
>   or take your Holy Spirit from me.
> Restore to me the joy of your salvation,
>   and grant me a willing spirit to sustain me.
> (Ps 51:3–12, NIV)

The fundamental concept here is that healing cannot be experienced until one confesses this guilt and asks for forgiveness, as is explicitly pointed out in Ps 32:

> As long as I would not speak, my bones wasted away
>   with my groaning all the day,
> For day and night your hand was heavy upon me;

> my strength was dried up as by the heat of summer.
> Then I acknowledged my sin to you,
>> my guilt I covered not.
> I said, "I confess my faults to the LORD,"
>> and you took away the guilt of my sin."
> (Ps 32:3–5, NAB)

In sharp contrast with the profound feelings of guilt expressed in Psalms such as 38, 51 and 32, there is another whole series of Psalms which represent a very different orientation. In this second group, the persons praying the psalms boldly affirm their innocence and even challenge God to test them and find out that they are in fact innocent:

> The Lord has dealt with me according to my righteousness;
>> according to the cleanness of my hands he has rewarded
>> me.
> For I have kept the ways of the Lord;
>> I have not done evil by turning from my God.
> All his laws are before me;
>> I have not turned away from his decrees.
> I have been blameless before him
>> and have kept myself from sin.
> The Lord has rewarded me according to my righteousness,
>> according to the cleanness of my hands in his sight.
> (Ps 18:20–24, NIV)

> Vindicate me, O Lord,
>> for I have led a blameless life;
> I have trusted in the Lord
>> without wavering.
> Test me, O Lord, and try me,
>> examine my heart and my mind;
> for your love is ever before me,
>> and I walk continually in your truth.
> I do not sit with deceitful men,

> nor do I consort with hypocrites;
> I abhor the assembly of evildoers
>   and refuse to sit with the wicked.
> (Ps 26:1–5, NIV)

Of course the classic statement of the innocence of the suffering person is not in the Psalms, but in Job. In that book, Job's associates try to convince him that his misfortunes, including his disease, must be due to sin on his part. Job, however, insists with dogged determination that such is not the case and that he is in fact innocent of any offense. When God finally speaks, towards the end of the book, we are assured that on this point Job was correct and his friends were wrong. The combination of the Book of Job and the psalms of innocence such as 7, 18 and 26, provide a powerful counterbalance to the view found in the Penitential Psalms.

The contrast between the confessions of guilt and the protestations of innocence provides interesting material for discussion. On some occasions, I have had a class read these two series of quotations aloud in unison and then asked students to comment on which type of statement they could most easily identify with. It usually turns out that some persons are more comfortable with the confessions of guilt while others identify more with the statements of innocence. Perhaps there are personality differences which incline people in either of the two directions, although I hasten to add that it does not seem that an objective observer would find that persons in the one group had any more or less reasons for feeling guilty than persons in the other group.

In such a discussion of guilt, it will be readily agreed that there are times when the guilt that we feel is not justified. It often happens in family situations, for example, that parents, children, or spouses ask of us something to which we must reply, "No." Even when that "No" is perfectly legitimate and appropriate, however, many people testify that they still feel guilty even though they know perfectly well in their rational minds that there is no reason why they should feel guilty. Most people agree, therefore, that in at least some instances the feelings of guilt which we have are unjustified and inappropriate. Nonetheless, we still need to find freedom from this guilt because it does form part of our dis-ease.

There are some psychologists who would go even further and argue that in fact feeling guilty is always unjustified and inappropriate, that it is by definition unhealthy. This view is shared by Dr. Gerald Jampolski, an M.D. who experienced a remarkable spiritual conversion in his own life and is now a holistic health practitioner. He believes that the healing of the relationship with God is an integral part of the therapeutic process. In his recent book *Goodbye to Guilt* he describes the crucial importance of handling guilt through the practice of forgiveness. However, Jampolski does not regard guilt as something "real" but as an "illusion" which is created by our misperception of reality. Another nationally recognized leader in the field of holistic medicine, Dr. Heather Morgan, of Dayton, Ohio, has a similar approach. She explains that according to her way of looking at the situation there are three stages in the religious understanding of forgiveness. In the first stage, we come to realize that whenever we turn to God and ask for forgiveness, we will always be forgiven. The second stage is the discovery that when we turn to God, we have already been forgiven. The third stage, she says, is the ultimate realization that in God's eyes there was never anything to forgive in the first place. The views of Jampolski and Morgan differ from traditional Christian theology, though it is by no means clear that they are incompatible with it.

In any case, whether or not we regard our feelings of guilt as justified, we can certainly agree with the Psalms that our healing from dis-ease requires that, in one way or another, we achieve freedom from guilt. Forgiveness is the process we go through in dealing with this guilt. However, before discussing forgiveness, it will be helpful to consider the related problem of "the enemies" in the Psalms.

The Problem of the Enemies

It was noted above that in the holistic perspective of the Old Testament, dis-ease involved a social dimension in which one not only felt alienation from friends, but also experienced being attacked by hostile parties which we can refer to as "the enemies." Complete wholeness can not be restored to an individual until the hostility of these enemies has been handled in some way. The perspective exhibited by the Psalms appears to view this whole aspect of things as a strictly "win/lose" alternative. If the person praying is to be vindicated, then the enemies must be humiliated and defeated. This attitude is due in part to the fact that many of these psalms seem to be referring to situations in which the enemies were actually attempting physical harm to the person through violent means. The use of force to overcome and subdue such attackers seemed to be the only possibility. There is another factor at play, however. I am referring to the concept of power and honor which prevailed in ancient Israel, as in the rest of the ancient world, and in fact appears to be characteristic of patriarchal societies. The attitude is that if someone ridicules and humiliates me, my honor has lost something which cannot be restored until the other party is humiliated and forced to acknowledge me. There is a vertical perspective in this understanding of power and the relationships between individuals. If someone has put me "down", then I really can not feel good about myself until I have (or God has) turned the tables on them. This is why, for example, Psalm 23, "The Lord is my shepherd," says in verse 5, "You spread the table before me in the sight of my foes

(NAB)." This very popular psalm, which in other respects reflects thoughts and attitudes so congenial to Christian devotion, is not able to picture the full vindication of the pious person without a reference to the enemies. These opponents must see the blessing received by God's servant so they will know whose side God is on and realize that they are the losers. Without their humiliation, the victory would not be complete!

With the prevalence of such attitudes, it is not surprising that along with prayers for God's help, the laments of the individual include imprecations, prayers for the defeat of the enemy, such as the following:

> Let their own table be a snare before them,
>   and a net for their friends.
> Let their eyes grow dim so that they cannot see,
>   and keep their backs always feeble.
> Pour out your wrath upon them;
>   let the fury of your anger overtake them.
> Let their encampment become desolate;
>   in their tents let there be no one to dwell.
> For they kept after him whom you smote,
>   and added to the pain of him you wounded.
> Heap guilt upon their guilt,
>   and let them not attain to your reward.
> May they be erased from the book of the living,
>   and not be recorded with the just!
> (Ps 69:23–29, NAB)

> Raise up a wicked man against him,
>   and let the accuser stand at his right hand.
> When he is judged, let him go forth condemned,
>   and may his plea be in vain.
> May his days be few;
>   may another take his office.
> May his children be fatherless,
>   and his wife a widow.

May his children be roaming vagrants and beggars;
may they be cast out of the ruins of their homes.
May the usurer ensnare all his belongings,
and strangers plunder the fruit of his labors.
May there be no one to do him a kindness,
nor anyone to pity his orphans.
He loved cursing; may it come upon him;
he took no delight in blessing; may it be far from him.
And may he be clothed with cursing as with a robe;
may it penetrate into his entrails like water
and like oil into his bones;
May it be for him like a garment which covers him,
like a girdle which is always about him.
(Ps 109:6–12, 17–19, NAB)

Other examples may be found in Pss 28:4–5; 35:4–8 and 137:8–9.

Modern readers of the Psalms are often uncomfortable with these imprecations and object that it is not right to give voice to the thoughts and feelings expressed in such passages. However, before claiming that we are somehow above all this anger and hostility, it might be a good idea to explore the possibility that deep inside of us we do harbor similar thoughts and feelings whose presence we deny because we are so strongly convinced that they are "not nice," or "not Christian." If we do have some of this negativity within us, then it is part of our dis-ease and it might be that in order to experience wholeness we must honestly face this dark side of ourselves and bring it out into the light where it can be healed.

A set of exercises which I use for working on this material centers on the creation of an "enemies list." As a warm-up process, I ask students to sit in groups of four or five. They are instructed to go around the circle several times, each completing the sentence, "One thing/person I resent is. . . ." These statements are to be very brief, with no explanation necessary. The idea is to go around the circle several times in rapid-fire succession. One can use variations like, "Sometimes I feel victimized by . . . ," or, "I am often in conflict with. . . ." After a few minutes of this, the thought process has been stimulated and the individual can sit down with a piece of paper to write out an itemized "enemies list." I assure them that they will not be asked to share what's on this list with anyone else and they can destroy it after the meeting is over if they want. I explain that the persons, situations or things they feel resentful about would be some of the enemies. Similarly with the feelings of being victimized and with the conflict situations. The list would probably include some people they deliberately keep away from as well as persons who are very close and very loved by them but with whom, in certain situations, they have a hostile relationship. It may be that we relate to some part of our personality as an enemy. Likewise, we may feel victimized by some part of our body or by a diseased organ, or by what we believe is the cause of our disease. For many of us, on the other hand, some of the enemies may be institutions. Finally, there may be occasions on which we view life itself, or nature, or even God, as the enemy.

With this preparation, we read aloud and in unison some of the imprecations against the enemies from the Psalms. I suggest to the group that some of them might feel reluctant to do this but that they might allow themselves to try it. After all, we are just reading some passages from the Bible! If some of the passages seem too terrible to be spoken about a person, then one could try thinking of the "institutional" enemies. After reading each passage, we have a silent pause to allow participants to observe what they are feeling right now or to switch the focus of their attention to a different "enemy." After the passages have all been read, we discuss what can be observed and learned from this process.

The discussion is very important because the learning that emerges from the exercise needs to be brought into conscious awareness. Moreover, it is beneficial for individuals to discover that other persons had reactions similar to their own. It is also advantageous for the group to see that not everyone had the same reactions. One of the most typical observations to come up is that of being very uncomfortable with the imprecations. Recognition of the discomfort provides an excellent opportunity to move to a deeper self-knowledge by exploring the uneasiness and discovering what gives rise to it. In some cases, persons come to the realization that they do not really wish ill to these "enemies," and they realize that the latter are actually doing the best they can in the situation. Such an awareness in itself can be a healing experience. In other cases it is acknowledged that the exercise puts persons in touch with feelings which have been repressed because they were conditioned to think that such feelings were "not nice." Group members who are coming from this position might be helped by other group members who, on the contrary, are both very much aware of and also comfortable with their hostile thoughts and feelings. Individuals in the latter category, in fact, sometimes share the fact that they enjoyed reading the imprecations and experienced a sense of power in uttering the curses.

There are other insights which can arise in the course of this discussion. On one occasion, a student shared that she was not comfortable pronouncing the imprecations against her own enemies, so she switched to saying them about persons who had treated her husband in such a way that she could regard them as his enemies. She had felt more comfortable after making this switch. As we talked about it, she realized that her reaction seemed to indicate that she thought it was acceptable to stand up for someone else (in this case, her husband), but that it was not acceptable to stand up for herself. In the light of the new insight, she could at least begin to ask herself whether she might not wish to become as assertive about her own rights as she was about somebody else's.

One man reported that the "enemy" he had in mind was a part of himself which he doesn't like. At first, he could really get into cursing and rejecting this part of himself. Suddenly he realized that wishing evil on a part of himself was the same as wishing evil on himself and he knew he really didn't want to do that. He would need to find a new way, other than rejection, for handling this part of himself.

Another woman said that during the exercise she was thinking of a person against whom she had held a grudge for a number of years. The anger she had about this other person often caused her considerable discomfort and tension. However, she did not want to let go of it because the other person had been so bad that she did not want to let that person "off the hook" by forgetting the anger. During the exercise, however, this student realized that the "punishment" produced by the anger was only harming herself and didn't affect the object of the anger who probably wasn't even aware of it any more. Thus she would only be helping herself by letting go of the anger and forgiving.

Whatever specific insights might arise in this discussion, there will usually be virtual unanimity that cursing one's enemies is not an effective way to attain healing and wholeness. It is my experience that even the persons who say they get relief by letting off steam in this way acknowledge that there is something more that needs to be done. The something more is that ultimately the enemies all need to be forgiven. Thus the problem of guilt, discussed in the previous section, falls together with the problem of the enemies in that the same solution applies to both.

Forgiveness

As the Psalms so clearly illustrate, it is not possible for us to experience complete healing until the problem posed by the presence of enemies has been resolved. The resolution of the problem, however, comes from a direction which is totally unexpected as long as we remain stuck in anger and hatred, unable to see further than the defeat and annihilation of the foe. The unexpected way is in fact the path of forgiveness. Its classic text is the statement of Jesus about those who nailed him to the cross: "Father, forgive them; for they know not what they do." (Lk 23:34 RSV) This forgiveness corresponds to the love of enemies proclaimed in Mt 5:43–45:

> You have heard that it was said, "You shall love your neighbor and hate your enemy." But I say to you, Love your enemies and pray for those who persecute you, so that you may be sons of your Father who is in heaven; for he makes his sun rise on the evil and on the good, and sends rain on the just and on the unjust. (RSV)

The path of love and forgiveness towards enemies leads to a result which is beautiful in its paradox: there are no more enemies! Their "annihilation" has come about, but in a manner which differs totally from the annihilation wished for during the moment of anger and hatred.

As I have already suggested, the solution to the problem of the enemies is linked to the solution of the problem of guilt. We say in the Lord's Prayer, "Forgive us our trespasses as we forgive those who trespass against us." The exegesis of this petition is provided by Mt 7:1–5:

> Judge not, that you be not judged. For with the judgment you pronounce you will be judged, and the measure you give will be the measure you get. Why do you see the

speck that is in your brother's eye, but do not notice the log that is in your own eye? Or how can you say to your brother, "Let me take the speck out of your eye," when there is the log in your own eye? You hypocrite, first take the log out of your own eye, and then you will see clearly to take the speck out of your brother's eye. (RSV)

Here the religious insight of the New Testament is in profound agreement with psychological understanding of the phenomenon of projection, the process by which we identify in other persons the qualities and characteristics which we cannot tolerate in ourselves, then project outward the judgment, rejection, anger and hatred which we secretly hold against ourselves.

The phenomenon of projection can be illustrated through a simple group process. Presuming the group has worked on the "enemies list" described above, ask them to pick out a person about whom they have especially strong negative feelings. Then, taking a blank sheet of paper, draw a vertical line down the middle. At the top of the left hand column, write the heading, "Character analysis of _____," with the name of a juicy "enemy" filled in. Then ask the participants to list all the qualities or characteristics of this person which produce feelings of anger, resentment and hatred. These character defects should be numbered consecutively and the longer the list the better. After five or ten minutes, instruct them to write their own names at the top of the right hand column, then opposite each item, write down, as honestly as they can, the extent to which the same characteristic is found in themselves. In some cases it might be "Just like me." In other cases, the similarity will seem to be slight or non-existent. After sufficient time has elapsed, have individuals share the results in small groups. A surprisingly large number will discover (sometimes as an unpleasant surprise) that what they hate in others is exactly what they hate in themselves.

In the case of persons who didn't find the presence of the hated character defects in themselves, it is possible that a further step would be helpful. Ask them how they would feel if they found these traits in themselves. Furthermore, ask them to consider as honestly as they can whether there might be some situations in which, unless they very carefully controlled their behavior, they could possibly become like the person they are thinking of. If they answer, "Yes," then it might be asked, "Is it possible that what you judge in that person is a projection of what you view as a *potential* evil in yourself? Could it be that the hostility you have towards that person is a strategy you have to prevent yourself from doing things for which you would find it difficult to forgive yourself?" With such suggestions, most persons in a group will attain, at least to some extent, an experiential grasp of projection.

As we become aware of how projection operates, we realize more and more that the judgments we pass on others are at one and the same time judgments which condemn us. By holding others guilty, we confirm the reality of guiltiness which then boomerangs. If we want to become free from guilt, the one identical forgiveness must be applied both to others and to ourselves. It is not just that God has arbitrarily decided to forgive us if and when we forgive others. The process is, in a sense, automatic: precisely insofar as we forgive our enemies, we too are liberated from guilt.

Just as, through much of our lives, we have made judging, rejecting and condemning a habit of mind, so too can we develop the opposite mental attitude of forgiveness. It is something we can practice and become more adept at. Consequently, in my workshops, I teach a forgiveness exercise which can be practiced on a regular basis. We begin, as usual, with a brief relaxation and centering process. Then with appropriate music in the background I continue:

> I would like you to think of some place from your past, preferably from your childhood, where you felt completely safe. It may be a room or a place outdoors. See yourself there as you were then. Let yourself see, hear, smell and feel the sensations you felt in that place. (Pause) Keeping in your body the sense of being in that place, imagine yourself there as an adult, just as you are today. Think of this as a place of forgiveness. Imagine forgiveness coming down onto this place in some way: perhaps a gentle rain of forgiveness showering down all over you; or golden flakes of forgiveness slowly drifting down; or a beam of warm forgiving light streaming over you. Let yourself be covered and totally penetrated by this forgiveness so that you become more and more aware of how totally and completely forgiven you are—so forgiven that you might think of yourself as being in a state of innocence and perfection. See how this feels to you. (Pause)

> I would like you now to think of someone you love and whom you find it very easy to forgive. Let this person enter your special space, this place of forgiveness. Let the forgiveness come down on this person too: showering down like gentle rain, or slowly descending in golden flakes of forgiveness or in a warm beam of forgiving light. This person too is totally immersed and suffused with forgiveness. (Pause) The two of you are aware of how totally forgiven you both are. Forgiven from above and forgiven by each other. How do you relate to one another in this awareness of your innocence and your perfection? Enjoy for a while what it feels like when persons who are totally forgiven are together. (Pause)

> Let the person who has been with you go now, slowly moving away and leaving you alone. And now I would like

you to allow someone from your "enemies list" to come into your special place, and let the forgiveness also shower down upon this person—falling like rain, or golden flakes or a warm beam of forgiving light. Let the forgiveness totally cover and penetrate this person. See if you can allow the forgiveness to come, not just from above, but from your heart too, moving out towards this person. What is it like to be with an "enemy" in the awareness that both of you are forgiven? (Pause) Gradually allow more and more people from your "enemies list" to enter this scene. See the forgiveness literally flooding down from above, soaking through and transforming everyone. Try saying to yourself, "Forgive us our trespasses as we forgive those who trespass against us." How does it feel to be part of a group of forgiven persons? (Pause)

I would now like you to prepare yourselves to return to the reality of this room. Take a deep breath then let it out. Now take another deep breath, and as you let it out, gently open your eyes.

The experiences which participants have in this visualization should be shared in small groups. For some individuals, it will be a powerful healing experience. Others will express frustration because they had a great resistance to allowing certain people into their special place and they were just not able to extend the forgiveness to them. These members of the group need to be reassured that learning to forgive is a process and it might not come to them all at once. However, it is possible to practice. If they repeat a visualization or meditation of this type on a regular basis, beginning with the persons who are easiest to forgive and then building up to the harder ones, they will probably find that the sense of healing which they discover will encourage them to move on and they will eventually be able to include everyone in their forgiveness.

At this point, we are about ready to move on to another matter. Before doing so, however, I would like to say a final word about the enemies in the Psalms. The view I have proposed is that we must move from the anger and hatred expressed in the imprecations against the enemies and learn to forgive. It would be wise, however, not to be too hasty in doing so. There is perhaps a danger that we might just deny and repress our hostile emotions under the illusion that we have achieved total forgiveness and that the violent feelings in some of the psalms are somehow beneath us. The great contribution of the Psalms in this connection is that they provide very honest and forthright expression to thoughts and attitudes which we might prefer not to look at. Sometimes theologians tend to dismiss the treatment of the enemies in the Psalms as a lower stage in the development of moral or ethical sensitivity. It is claimed that Christianity has achieved a higher ethical perspective, a purer morality, which would forbid Christians from praying certain passages from the psalter. Might it not be healthier to view those uncomfortable passages in the Psalms as part of a process which all human beings go through, no matter how highly developed their sense of ethics or morality? By viewing the matter in this way, we can allow ourselves to go through that phase of the process, while at the same time we make sure that we don't get stuck there. Such an attitude would probably be more helpful in the promotion of our own healing.

Visualizing Our Wholeness

There is a feature which occurs in a number of the laments of the individual which we have not yet adequately paid attention to. In some of these psalms we find after a section of characteristic lament or complaint an abrupt change of mood. The

worshipper seems to jump into the expression of praise as if
the prayer had already been answered. For example, in Psalm
22 there is a long passage containing the most intense and bit-
ter lament. Then we find in verses 23–25:

> I will proclaim your name to my brethren;
>> in the midst of the assembly I will praise you:
> "You who fear the LORD, praise him;
>> all you descendants of Jacob, give glory to him;
>> revere him, all you descendants of Israel!
> For he has not spurned nor disdained
>> the wretched man in his misery,
> Nor did he turn his face away from him,
>> but when he cried out to him, he heard him (NAB)."

The quotation marks enclosing the words of praise which are
used in the NAB translation cited above, suggest the interpretation that these are the words which will be sung after the
prayer has been answered. One should note, however, that
ancient Hebrew did not have any quotation marks, so their use
in the English is the translators' way of handling the difficulty
posed by the presence of "anticipatory" words of praise in what
otherwise seems to be a lament. There are other psalms of lament, however, where the incongruity can not be so easily
smoothed over. In Psalm 6, verses 2–8 complain about intense
physical and emotional distress which has brought the worshipper to the very brink of death. Then all of a sudden we find
in verses 9–10:

> Depart from me, all evildoers,
>> for the LORD *has heard* the sound of my weeping.
> The LORD *has heard* my plea;
>> the LORD *has accepted* my prayer.
> (NAB, emphasis added)

Similarly in Psalm 28 the psalmist is pleading to be delivered from death. There is a short imprecation against the enemies. Then quite abruptly:

> Blessed be the LORD;
>> for he *has heard* the sound of my pleading;
>> the LORD is my strength and my shield.
> In him my heart trusts, and I find help;
>> then my heart exults, and with my song I give him
>>> thanks.
> (NAB, emphasis added) Ps 28:6–7

Biblical scholarship has proposed a theory to account for the unexpected change of mood represented by this kind of "anticipatory praise." These psalms were apparently used as part of a ritual in the temple. At a certain point in the liturgy, it was the priest's function to announce, in the name of God, that this person's prayer had been heard. This announcement, which scholars call the "priestly oracle of salvation," is not preserved in the text of the psalm because it was spoken by the priest, and not by the person praying the psalm. Though the intervention of a priestly oracle of salvation is only a theory, it seems to be the most reasonable explanation of the phenomenon we have been describing.

How does this help us understand the process of healing? What it seems to mean is that there is a transition point at which it may appear from all outward evidence that the individual is still in the state of dis-ease, but nonetheless there is a sense in which the healing has already taken place. This state of affairs, reflected in the psalms, corresponds to reports made by persons who have experienced healing in dramatic ways. These persons often state that they came to a point where they "knew" they had been healed within and that it was just a matter of time before that would manifest itself in external ways.

Also, in the literature on the use of visualization in healing, there is much to suggest that insofar as we think of ourselves as sick, we manifest sickness in our bodies; but if we visualize ourselves as whole, the external reality moves in the direction of that wholeness. All of this suggests the way in which a modern counterpart can be found for the function of the priestly salvation oracle in the psalms. We no longer have a ritual involving a priest who is authorized to transmit divine assurance that our prayers have been heard. But we can visualize!

The visualization which I use begins by asking participants to sit up with their spines straight, both feet on the floor and eyes closed. I then say:

> Take a few deep breaths, consciously relaxing your body as you exhale. Let your shoulders and arms just hang loosely. Let go of any tension in your facial muscles, dropping all expression from your face. Let this relaxation move down through your upper body, your thighs and legs, all the way to your feet. (Pause) Keep your breath regular and a little deeper than normal and bring your attention to your incoming breath. Just observe this inbreath. (Pause) Now I want you to follow this in-breath and let it lead you inside yourself. Each breath takes you deeper within yourself. You are moving towards that vital creative place deep inside of you, the center where you find the power of healing. (Pause) At this deep inner center, I want you to visualize a small sphere of intense white light. Become fully aware of this; feel its warmth; see its light. Each time you inhale, allow the intensity of the light and warmth to increase. (Brief pause) Now with each incoming breath, let the sphere of white healing light slowly begin to get bigger and bigger. (Brief pause) As it grows, let it begin to fill your body. Your whole torso begins to be filled with the radiating energy of this light. It begins to expand into your arms and legs and through your neck, into your head. Your whole body is filling up with warm,

bright healing light. And as it moves through your body it is healing every part of your body which needs healing. Be especially aware of the areas which you associated with your dis-ease in our earlier work. Let the healing energy bring wholeness to these parts. Let it also heal your feelings and your mind. Though we are not here trying to change other persons, let the light heal your relationships insofar as they are a part of you which needs healing. (Pause) Be aware now of how radiant and resplendent you are with the bright light of healing which has brought you into a state of wholeness. Imagine yourself being as fully healed, as fully made whole as you could wish or picture yourself to be. What does it feel like to you to be healed, to be in your wholeness? (Pause) If you were like this all the time, how might you think, act and feel differently from what you have been used to so far? (Pause) In a moment, now, I am going to ask you to return to the reality of this room. But I would like you to do it slowly and gently so that you bring back with you as much as is possible of the sense of wholeness that you have been imaging. So try wiggling your toes and your fingers just a little. Take a few deep breaths. Stretch your body in whatever way it wants to stretch. Then when you are ready, gently open your eyes.

It is important that the experience of this powerful visualization process be reinforced by either having everyone share some aspect of it in small groups or having at least a number of the participants verbalize the experience in the larger group. Many, if not all, of the participants will have experienced at least to some degree a very pleasant sensation of being already healed. As group leader, what I try to reinforce is the concept that if we can experience our healing and our wholeness in a visualization, that can only take place because in some sense we already are healed and whole. I also emphasize that this experience of wholeness is not something which

I, as group leader, produced in them, but something which they themselves produced with only a few suggestions from me, suggestions which they could reproduce for themselves in a variety of ways whenever they want to. Finally, I recommend the regular practice of a visualization of this sort in the belief that wholeness is in some ways a habit of mind which can be developed by practice and attention just as surely as misery can be indulged by the practice of complaining and negativity.

There is a "homework" assignment which can be used as a follow-up to this visualization process. One draws a vertical line down the middle of a sheet of blank paper. In the left hand column, itemize as many details as can be remembered from the last part of the visualization where it was asked, "If you were in this state all the time, how might you think, feel and act differently?" The more specific details one can add, the better. Afterwards, note in the right hand column which of these thoughts, feelings and behaviors could *already* be practiced without waiting for some dramatic future arrival of wholeness. Realizing how many of these things (perhaps even all of them!) can be done right now, we strengthen the conviction that we have in a sense already been healed. And, of course, by feeling, thinking, and acting as persons who are aware of their wholeness, we move further and further along the way of manifesting wholeness in our lives.

Returning Praise

Any group which has followed the steps outlined in this chapter all the way to this point deserves a celebration. And a celebration is exactly what the ancient Israelite rituals provide for!

As was pointed out earlier, an integral part of the lament of the individual was the vow to return praise after the prayer had been answered. So when in fact sick persons had been healed, they would return to the temple to fulfill this vow. There is a special genre of psalm which was used on such occasions, namely, the thanksgiving psalm of the individual (for example, Pss 9, 18, 30, 32, 92, 116, and 138). In these psalms the worshipper would look back upon the crisis in retrospect, often quoting the words of lament which had been used during the time of need. Then came the heart of the matter, the declaration that God had heard the prayer and intervened to help the worshipper. As a result, the individual praises God and invites all by-standers to join in the praise and thanksgiving. Along with the praise in word and song went participation in a communion sacrifice in which food and drink were shared by the worshipper's family and friends. These festal meals are referred to in Psalm 22:26 (verse 27 in the Hebrew text), "The afflicted shall eat and be satisfied; those who seek him shall praise the Lord (RSV)." The drink which was shared is alluded to in Ps 116:13, "I will lift the cup of salvation and call upon the name of the Lord."

The information about the thanksgiving ritual which has just been summarized provides a wonderful model for concluding a group's work on dis-ease and healing in the psalms. One of the thanksgiving psalms of the individual, Psalm 116, lends itself admirably to use in this context. A few preparations will need to be taken care of. Each group member should go through the laments of the individual and pick out one verse of lament which applies to the way he or she experienced the situation of dis-ease. Also, each person should either pick out a psalm verse or compose an original statement which represents the way in which he or she experienced healing, for example, "God drew me up, the light dawned upon me." These statements of lament and of healing will be inserted at appropriate places in Psalm 116. A final matter which needs to be taken care of beforehand is arranging to bring food and drink to share, including a festive cup or goblet for wine, fruit juice or sparkling mineral water.

The ritual itself should take place in a suitable location and it might be better if this were not the classroom. All could stand in a circle with the food in the center and the goblet filled with whatever drink is being used. After a few moments of silence, all recite Ps 116 in unison according to the following form:

> I love the Lord for hearing my cry for help,
>> because God's ear inclined to me when I cried out.
>
> The cords of death surrounded me,
>> the snares of the underworld were upon me,
>> I came into affliction and grief.
>
> (Each person in turn adds a statement of lament.)
>
> I called on the name of the Lord,
>> "O Lord, save my life!"
>
> The Lord is gracious and upright,
>> our God is merciful.
>
> The Lord guards the little ones.
>> I was brought low and God rescued me.
>
> Return to your serenity, O my soul,
>> for the Lord is generous with you.
>
> God freed my life from death,
>> my eyes from weeping,
>> and my feet from stumbling.
>
> I will walk in the presence of the Lord,
>> in the lands of the living.
>
> What can I give back to the Lord,
>> in gratitude for what I have received?
>
> I will lift the cup of salvation,
>> and call upon the name of the Lord;
>
> I will fulfill my vows to the Lord,
>> in the company of God's people.

(Each in turn takes the cup, making a statement about the
    healing which has been experienced.)
O Lord, I am indeed your servant,
    your servant, a child of your servants.
    You have loosened my bonds.
In praise, I will share a communion sacrifice,
    and call upon the name of the Lord.
I will fulfill my vows to the Lord,
    in the company of God's people.
Within the enclosure of the Lord's house,
    In your midst, O Jerusalem. (Ps 116:1–9,12–14,16–19)

At this point a joyful hymn of praise which everyone knows can
be sung. Then food and drink are shared. The celebration may
appropriately be ended with the kiss of peace.

NOTE

1. There are many excellent books on Psalms written by schol-
ars but in a popular style. Some of the more recent ones are: B. W.
Anderson, *Out of the Depths: The Psalms Speak for Us Today*. Rev.
ed. (Philadelphia: Westminster Press, 1983); W. Brueggemann, *The
Message of the Psalms: A Theological Commentary* (Minneapolis:
Augsburg, 1984); J. F. Craghan, *The Psalms: Prayers for the Ups,
Downs and In-Betweens of Life* (Wilmington, Del.: 1984); C. Wes-
termann, *The Psalms: Structure, Content & Message* (Minneapolis:
Augsburg, 1980). An important, but more technical, contribution is
C. Westermann, *Praise and Lament in the Psalms* (Atlanta: John
Knox Press, 1981).

Appendix

Historical Criticism and Beyond

In the introduction to *Life Journey and the Old Testament* I noted that the field of biblical scholarship is dominated by what is referred to as the historico-critical method. The Appendix now turns to a detailed discussion of this historico-critical approach. As such, it will serve to locate *Life Journey and the Old Testament* within a broader context. Readers who are not trained in biblical studies will gain a clearer understanding of what is meant by historical criticism. On the other hand, biblical scholars and theologians will learn what I mean by speaking of the limitations of the critical approach and why it is necessary to move beyond it. I hope that this Appendix will make a positive contribution to the ongoing debate concerning hermeneutics and the nature of biblical scholarship.

1. The Historico-Critical Method

Throughout *Life Journey and the Old Testament,* the terms "historical criticism," "historico-critical method," and "the critical approach," are used synonymously and in a broad sense. They designate the whole complex made up of the more narrowly defined methodologies such as textual criticism, literary criticism and form criticism. There are also some newer methodologies such as structuralism which sometimes claim to transcend historical criticism. From my point of view, however, even these newer methodologies approach the Bible from a detached and descriptive perspective which falls short of relating scholarship to the existential concerns of human persons. In this book, therefore, all the descriptive methodologies are included under the umbrella of historical criticism.

Towards a Definition.   The historico-critical method is so broad and diverse that it cannot easily be captured within a concise definition. However, a workable description can be attained by delineating the method from a variety of aspects. To begin with, historical criticism is the method used by persons who are recognized in the academic world as scholars in the field. This includes professors in state universities, or other secular colleges and universities, as well as in the colleges and seminaries related to the Roman Catholic Church and the mainline Protestant denominations. In other words, employment of the historico-critical method is the standard practice in the academic study of religion, with the exception of a few schools associated with Fundamentalist churches which decry the historico-critical approach as the antithesis of what biblical study should be. It follows that in the professional organizations of scholars (the so-called "learned societies" such as the Society of Biblical Literature, the American Academy of Religion, and the Catholic Biblical Association) it is the historico-critical point of view which is expressed in the papers delivered, in discussions, and in the publications.

One way, then, of identifying the historico-critical way of studying the Bible is to think of it as the approach which is used in academic circles in contrast to the way the Bible is used in churches and synagogues. In fact, such a manner of viewing the situation corresponds quite well to the way in which the historico-critical point of view emerged historically. In ancient times and through the Middle Ages, the task of expounding the meaning of the Bible was carried on by religious authorities. Each religious group brought its own beliefs to the study of the Bible as a set of presuppositions. It was taken for granted that what one would find in the Bible would correspond to what the church or synagogue had traditionally taught. If debate arose concerning the meaning of a passage, the argument could be settled by appeal to traditional authorities such as the church fathers or the rabbis. During the seventeenth century, however, a movement began which could be described as the liberation of biblical studies from the domination of religious authorities. Rather than in church or synagogue, it was in the arena of the free exchange of ideas that researchers would carry on their own independent investigations. Needless to say, these first historico-critical scholars often came into conflict with religious authorities. For example, during the 17th century, the French Catholic priest Richard Simon was forced to leave his religious order and the Jewish writer Baruch Spinoza was kicked out of his synagogue. Both of them had questioned the traditional teaching that Moses was the author of the first five books of the Bible.

The label used in reference to the academic study of the Bible which developed since the seventeenth century contains the words "historical" and "critical." By turning our attention to the meaning of these two words, we can arrive at an understanding of much of what is involved in the historico-critical method.

The method is historical in that it tries to abstract from the way in which biblical texts are understood by any given group of believers today, or the way in which Old Testament texts were interpreted in New Testament times. Instead the material is restored to the original historical context in which it developed. For example, the texts in Isaiah 40–55, so-called Second Isaiah, are better understood when one realizes that they were written after the destruction of Jerusalem in 587 B.C. and that they were addressed as a message of consolation to the Jewish exiles in Babylon. This section of the book of Isaiah, then, could not have been authored by the prophet Isaiah who was mentioned in the early chapters of the book and who lived in Jerusalem towards the end of the eighth century B.C. Another example is the Emmanuel prophecy of Isaiah 7:14 which must be seen in the light of the international situation of its time, when Assyria was expanding its empire and the kings of Samaria and Damascus were trying to force Judah to help them in an anti-Assyrian coalition. When seen in that historical context, the prophecy that "the young woman is pregnant and will bear a son and call him Emmanuel," must be understood as referring originally to a child who would be born very soon after the utterance of the prophecy. The historico-critical approach, therefore, makes us aware that the original meaning of certain texts differs considerably from what they were later understood to mean.[1]

The element "critical," on the other hand, is derived from a Greek root which means "to judge, evaluate, decide." The critic does not unquestioningly accept the view of a teacher or of a tradition, but examines the available evidence and attempts to "judge, evaluate, decide," on the basis of that evidence. All questions are considered legitimate. In fact, the more questions one raises the better. The truth will emerge from the free spirit of inquiry and the free exchange of ideas rather than from conservatively clinging to what people said about it in the past.

Objective and Scientific?   Sometimes, persons who are in favor of the historico-critical approach claim on its behalf that it is "the objective way of studying the Bible." On the other hand, those who reject historico-critical study (these are often representatives of more conservative religious traditions) like to try to demonstrate that in fact the method is not purely objective. I believe the truth of the matter requires more nuanced expression. First of all, if objective is taken to mean "purely objective" without any presuppositions whatsoever, then it must be recognized that there are no human statements, including the results of historico-critical study of the Bible, which are objective in this sense. The academic study of the Bible accepts many of the same presuppositions as have to be accepted in any other branch of historical study. We have to assume that the reactions of human beings to a given set of conditions in ancient times are similar to how people would react in analogous situations today. For example, both then and now, power-hungry individuals might decide to overthrow a weak government in order to attain their own ends. This principle of historical analogy has to be presupposed, otherwise we would not be able to understand history at all. So it is freely granted that the historico-critical approach is not "purely objective" in the sense of being without presuppositions. On the other hand, though, there does seem to be a more restricted sense in which the method does attain a good measure of objectivity. For example, researchers are often able to set aside, at least temporarily, their own religious beliefs regarding some issue, in order to look at the evidence in a detached way. So in spite of the fact that Jewish and Christian tradition had for centuries agreed that Moses was the author of the first five books (the Pentateuch), practitioners of a historico-critical approach were able to conclude that such was not the case. The fact that historico-critical scholars coming from a variety of religious traditions unanimously agree on this matter testifies that the method is able to bring investigators together in spite of ideological boundaries which separate them. It is not too much, then, to want to use the label "objective" to describe this phenomenon. Moreover, the method is objective in the sense that the presuppositions which enter into the study of the Bible are the same as the presuppositions used to study any other similar literature. One might compare the case of a woman who is evaluating the skill of young ballet dancers, one of whom is her own son. She is surely not without presuppositions, for she has very concrete ideas of what constitutes excellence in dancing (not "purely objective"). These presuppositions include concepts and ideas as well as factors relating to value and feeling. At the same time, she might possibly be the kind of person who can apply these criteria fairly to all the contestants, without favoring her own son. The very special relationship and feeling she has for him would not be allowed to enter into the evaluation of the dancing. Though such detachment is difficult to attain and many of us would disqualify ourselves from the judges' panel, it is nonetheless possible. Would it not be legitimate to assert that such a person merits the designation "objective"?

Furthermore, the historico-critical method is scientific in the sense that it is open to questioning and will settle matters on the basis of observable evidence. It will create hypotheses which are to be tested against the data. Given the nature of the material being studied, however, it cannot be scientific in the same sense as disciplines such as physics and chemistry.

God, Miracles and Inspiration.   One of the distinctive features of the historico-critical method is that it does not allow itself to use God as the explanation for anything. Of course practitioners of the discipline do talk about God since it is impossible not to do so when discussing religious literature such as the Bible. The point is that if they are speaking strictly as historico-critical scholars, they will make only descriptive statements, that is, statements which *describe* what the Bible says about God or what the people of biblical times believed about God. For example, one might say, "The Bible teaches that it was God, Yahweh, who redeemed the Israelite slaves from bondage in Egypt." Speaking as a historico-critical scholar, however, one remains neutral as to the truth or falsity of such a belief. When giving a strictly historico-critical answer to the question "How did the Israelite slaves get out of Egypt?" the critic must stick to natural, rational explanations and is not allowed to say "God did it." One way of describing this state of affairs is by using the traditional theological concepts of primary and secondary causality. According to this teaching, God is the primary cause of everything that happens. At the same time, there are secondary or more immediate causes which can be studied rationally or scientifically. When people say that "God sends the rain," they are speaking in terms of primary causality. Such a statement is not contradicted if a meteorologist explains the cause of the rain in terms of relative humidity, atmospheric pressure, and the movement of air masses (i.e. secondary causality). In this sense, we can say that historico-critical study of the Bible, since it is attempting to be scientific, concerns itself only with the level of secondary causality.

The fact that scholars, when they are speaking strictly as exponents of historico-critical study, avoid using God as an explanation, does not necessarily mean that such persons are not personally religious. In fact, the great majority of historico-critical scholars are believers. Their situation may be compared to that of a chemist who believes in God and is personally deeply religious. As long as he is in the laboratory, thinking and speaking strictly as a chemist, he must give scientific explanations for things. If a student asks him why certain chemicals combine in a certain way, he cannot get away with an answer like "God does it." He must remain on the level of secondary causality and give a rational explanation. The same person, however, perhaps after leaving the laboratory, may allow himself to step aside from his strictly scientific role and say that as a believer, he stands in awe of the mystery of the universe as it is revealed in atomic and molecular structures, and that these wonders speak to him of the God he believes in.

It might be objected that limiting oneself to a scientific study of secondary causes without attention to some role of God in the process is legitimate in chemistry but does not apply to the study of the Bible. Those of us who have a personal religious commitment and have chosen to employ the historico-critical method believe that our intelligence, our ability to think things out rationally, is a divine gift which we are meant to use to the best of our ability. The study of the Bible is no exception to this rule. Furthermore, as we apply historico-critical methods to the study of the biblical tradition, the understanding which we gain seems so cogent and clarifies so many problems, that the venture seems fully justified.

If a miracle is understood as a situation in which the secondary order of causality has been suspended and in which God has directly intervened to make something unique happen, then it is not surprising that miracles should pose a problem for a historico-critical approach. If such interruptions of secondary causality do in fact occur, then they are by definition outside of the scope of scientific inquiry. One could only say, "I cannot explain that, it is outside the realm of historico-critical explanation." In fact, some scholars who use historico-critical methods take precisely such an attitude to some of the reports found in the Bible, for example, the stories of the resurrection of Jesus. However, even if one believes in miracles in the sense described above, the momentum of being engaged in a process which is looking only at natural or rational explanations will have an effect on how miracle stories are viewed. In the case of any given story, an individual could speculate, "Perhaps in this specific case, what happened was purely natural and rationally understandable, but a legend grew up around it, depicting it in terms which seem miraculous." Here the principle of objectivity discussed above comes into play. For it must be admitted that if we were studying the religious literature of some other group of people (Greeks, Egyptians, Native Americans, etc.) such a possibility would have to be seriously entertained. The historico-critical method requires that the same questioning attitude, the same skepticism, must be applied to biblical stories. Let me therefore attempt to describe the state of affairs as I see it. If miracles are defined as above, a by-passing of ordinary secondary causality, there are many practitioners of historico-critical study who believe in the possibility of such miracles, though they would not automatically assume that every miracle story in the Bible is a factual report of a miracle in the strict sense. Another group of scholars would tend to completely deny the existence of such miracles. Yet others would revise the definition of miracle in such a way as to avoid the concept that secondary causality is suspended. In this approach, an event which, on the one hand, is capable of natural explanation, is at the same time such a powerful occasion for the experiencing of the divine mystery of the universe that it is said to deserve the designation "miracle." The latter position, while it preserves belief in the existence of miracles, agrees with the general historico-critical tendency to be skeptical about reports of events which defy the usual laws of nature. My own view is that recent developments in science, especially in the field of medicine and healing, should make us wary of too much self-assurance about what is or is not possible according to the laws of nature. We can therefore be open to the possibility that some of the biblical stories accurately preserve the records of unique and marvelous happenings. At the same time, it is perfectly legitimate for us to try to find natural explanations whenever that is possible.

The term "inspiration" refers to the idea that the biblical literature comes from God in some way. Inspiration, therefore, is usually explained as some kind of influence which God had upon the human writers of the Bible. Of course, according to the concepts of primary and secondary causality described above, it could be said that God, as primary cause, had an influence on the production of *any* piece of literature. Most theologians who speak of inspiration, however, would insist that it refers to something more than God's activity as primary cause and that the Bible comes from God in a special and unique way. The most rigid view of inspiration would be that the Bible was dictated by God word for word and that the human author acted only as a secretary, writing down these words. A somewhat more flexible, but still rather conservative, approach is to say that God put the ideas into the mind of the human author, but the latter was responsible for choosing the words to express these ideas. Yet another view is that inspiration is a kind of divine guidance which is limited to preventing the author from error concerning matters of essential belief.

Whatever the specific theory involved, it will be clear that reference to the phenomenon of inspiration amounts to using God as an explanation (viz., of how this literature originated). It follows from what was said above that scholars, insofar as they are operating precisely as historico-critical investigators, must set aside any consideration of inspiration. This does not mean such scholars personally reject inspiration. In fact, most biblical scholars do hold some theory of inspiration, although from a methodological point of view they do not bring that element into their critical discussions.

One way of looking at the debate over inspiration is to see it in terms of the relationship between the human factor and the divine factor in the origin of the Bible. In the more rigid doctrines of inspiration, such as the dictation theory, the human element is almost completely crowded out by the divine—the only human contribution is to write down the words dictated by God. Such a rigid perspective hardly allows scope for historico-critical investigation which focuses on the human factor rather than the divine. An example of an approach to inspiration which is more compatible with historico-critical study may be found in contemporary Roman Catholic thought. Here theologians have effectively used the analogy between the human and the divine in Christ. The traditional understanding has always been that Christ is fully human and fully divine. The divine does not take away any of the human. So if experts in anatomy had examined Jesus during his lifetime, they would have found everything that one finds in any human body—fully human. The purely biological examination, of course, would not be competent to say anything about the divine element. Analogously, it is possible to have a theology of inspiration in which the divine factor in the aetiology of the Bible is seen as compatible with the Bible's being fully human. Whatever is humanly characteristic of other literature and other authors is also true of the Bible. This does not say anything for or against the presence of a divine factor. A more flexible approach, then, allows free rein for the historico-critical study of the human aspect by recognizing that whatever inspiration actually is, it does not remove or reduce the humanity of the Bible.

Historical-Critical Method and the Churches. One of the central and persistent elements in the history of historico-critical study is the relentless state of controversy which has existed between the critics and the representatives of ecclesiastical orthodoxy. Pre-critical orthodoxy tended to see the truth as a monolithic whole which could be organized into a coherent system. The group's belief structure was thought to be identical with that found in the Bible (in spite of the fact that at any given time, there were different groups with different theologies, each claiming biblical validation). The Bi-

ble, as read by each denomination, was understood in such a
way as to support that denomination's beliefs. That the Bible
was read "pre-critically" means that claims which the Bible
makes about itself were taken at face value as representing
fact. For example, since the New Testament refers to the first
five books of the Old Testament (the Pentateuch) as the books
of Moses, it was believed that Moses did in fact write those
books. Stories such as Adam and Eve or the Flood were presumed to be historical accounts. Since the book of Isaiah begins with a rubric saying "The vision which Isaiah, the son of
Amoz, had. . . ." it was assumed that everything in that book
represented the words of Isaiah the son of Amoz. The book of
Daniel's claim to report the words and visions of a person who
had lived in the 6th century B.C. was accepted as true and,
consequently, the detailed symbolic representation of events
which took place in the 4th through 2nd centuries constituted
a prediction of future events which brilliantly illustrated the
divinely given fore-knowledge enjoyed by the prophets.

What a blow was delivered to the pre-critical mentality!
For the conclusions reached by critical investigation, and
which are accepted today by all practitioners of historico-critical scholarship shattered traditional views. The Pentateuch,
for example, is not the work of one person but a composite put
together from a number of sources, most of which are sub-
stantially later than the time of Moses. The early stories in
Genesis are adaptations of myths and legends which circulated
in Mesopotamia and elsewhere many centuries before the rise
of Israel. They express religious truths in a metaphorical way,
but are not historically factual accounts. The book of Isaiah
contains religious poetry and other literary material from a variety of authors whose activity spanned 4 or 5 centuries. In particular, as noted above, the section in chapters 40–55 was
written by an anonymous prophet who addressed the needs of
the Babylonian exiles about 150 years after the death of that

"Isaiah, the son of Amoz" mentioned at the beginning of the book. Finally, the book of Daniel was written during the second century B.C. and most of its "prophecies" were composed after the fact.

If these specific examples are not enough, let us consider some of the broader ramifications of critical biblical studies. By asserting that the Bible did not really say what the representatives of orthodox theology believed it said, the rug was pulled out from under the position that the denomination's orthodoxy was the same monolithic truth which went back to biblical times. In fact, critical studies demonstrated time and again that even within the Bible itself there is a variety of theological and religious ideas representing the thoughts of different persons and groups of persons over a long span of time. Many of these ideas, moreover, are similar, if not identical to ideas found in the religious literature of other people in the ancient world. How then could one continue to assert that the Bible was the unique revelation of God's eternal truth?

Within the Protestant denominations, it was especially in the 19th century that the great battles over these issues were fought. The denominations and theologians who accepted and came to terms with the critical approach became known as the representatives of "Liberalism." The conservatives, many of whom would today be labelled "Fundamentalists", clung to the old pre-critical view and denounced Liberalism and biblical criticism as a total betrayal of the faith. The dichotomy continues to exist to this day.

In the Roman Catholic Church, the process was different. In spite of the fact that a number of Catholic writers made important contributions to the early development of the historico-critical movement in the 17th and 18th centuries, the direction they pointed to was not followed. During the 19th century, critical scholarship was largely a Protestant enterprise while the pre-critical stance was maintained among

Catholics. Early in the twentieth century, there was a prom-
ising start at developing a historico-critical movement among
Catholics. Some of the most notable contributors to this movement were Père Marie-Joseph Lagrange and other French
Dominicans at the Ecole Biblique in Jerusalem. However,
when Roman ecclesiastical authorities began to react against
the movement known as Modernism, which was perceived as
a heretical threat to the faith, the incipient development of a
Catholic participation in critical biblical study was eradicated.

Finally, in 1943, Pope Pius XII issued a document entitled *Divino afflante spiritu* in which he gave the green light
for Catholics to pursue historico-critical study of the Bible.
This point of view has since been reiterated in official Church
pronouncements, especially in the document *De revelatione*
promulgated in 1965 by the Second Vatican Council. As a con-
sequence of these developments, the official position of the
Roman Catholic Church is on the side of recognizing the validity of historico-critical study and rejecting Fundamentalism. Paradoxically, Protestants, who were ahead of Catholics
in integrating the critical perspective, continue to be divided
on the issue.

While it is true that the official Roman Catholic position
endorses historico-critical study, honesty requires us to point
out that the endorsement is hedged with considerable caution.
There is in fact a great range of possible variations within the
spectrum of how one applies the critical methodologies. To
take an analogy from the medical field: most doctors would
agree that surgery is a legitimate therapeutic procedure; however, some doctors are extremely cautious and would use surgery only as a last resort if everything else failed, while others
would make much freer use of it. The "method" is the same
except that some use it more conservatively, others use it in a
more radical way. The use of historical-critical methods is analogous. There are more conservative critics and more radical

critics. Take for example the story of the Exodus, the escape of Israelite slaves from Egypt in the time of Moses. The majority of historico-critical scholars would agree that the account is based upon historical facts but also includes legendary elements. Within this consensus there is a wide range of possibilities. The more conservative view would be that the story is essentially historical, with a little addition of embellishment to improve the story in the telling. A more radical view might take the whole account as essentially legendary with such superficial basis in fact that the historical "nugget" can't even be recovered anymore. In situations such as this, the guardians of orthodoxy tend to favor the more conservative side of the spectrum. This conservative predisposition has not affected Old Testament scholarship significantly in recent years, but a number of theologians have been in conflict with the Vatican concerning the interpretation of the New Testament, especially in what it says about Jesus.

The information concerning the Catholic Church's acceptance of the historico-critical perspective comes as a surprise to some persons, both Catholic and non-Catholic. The reason for this is that we are still in a state of transition. The official go-ahead did not come until the 1940s. It took a while before persons could be trained in historico-critical techniques and then go on to teach in seminaries and universities. As a result of this time-lapse, priests who were in the seminary in the 1940s and, to some extent, even in the 1950s, were trained in the older theology. When younger priests emerged with a different educational background, the older men, who often had the position of pastor, might or might not be open to the new ideas. A similar situation existed with nuns, although on the whole they have had a stronger commitment to ongoing continuing education. Often the sisters were the first to bring knowledge of the newer approaches to the parish, only to be resisted by pastors and lay people. The effect of the latter is not to be underestimated. As a teacher of religious educators I have heard many stories of how sisters and brothers have tried to teach from a critical perspective, only to have parents come in and complain that their children were not being taught the "old time religion." Because we are in a time of transition, then, there is often a gap between what the biblical scholars are saying and what has gotten to the level of pastors and religious educators. Often an additional gap exists between the latter and the persons who sit in the pews. Nevertheless, a change is taking place, gradual though it may be. The change is observable in freshman college classes where a survey of students usually indicates that the majority of young people who went to Catholic elementary and secondary schools were taught from a critical point of view. For the others, one suspects that it is not so much that they were taught the pre-critical position, but rather that these questions were avoided in order not to stir up controversy.

2. The Positive Contributions of Historico-Critical Study

We are nearly at the point where we will examine the limitations of the historico-critical method with a view to moving beyond. Before doing that, however, I believe it is very important to say something about the benefits of historico-critical study so that the criticisms which can be made of it will appear in the proper context.

Among these positive benefits of the historico-critical enterprise, one of the most significant, paradoxically, arises precisely from the destructive impact which critical scholarship has had upon the dogmatic pre-critical theological systems. For those churches and theologians who have been open to the critical approach, the upsetting of old certitudes prepared the way for fresh and creative ways of theological expression in a climate of freedom and pluralism. A striking example of such a development is the case of Roman Catholic theology which has undergone an extraordinary revitalization in the wake of the Second Vatican Council, which met in the 1960s. It was the pioneering work of Catholic biblical scholars which, more than any other factor, cleared the ground and laid the foundations for the far-reaching changes in attitudes and reformulations of theology which emerged from the council. Since then it has continued to be the case that the most exciting and challenging new developments in Catholic theology have sought to ground themselves in historico-critical biblical studies.

A key aspect of such theological developments is a movement towards a more inclusive theology. It is freely admitted that historico-critical scholars have their own ways of being doctrinaire and intolerant. The method itself, however, has a powerful tendency to erode the parochial concept that the religious tradition, or denomination, or school of theology with which one is allied has an exclusive claim to truth. As critical scholars of different Christian denominations work harmoniously together, they learn respect for one another and often give up the need to prove that "my church is superior to yours." Similarly, a more sympathetic understanding of Judaism is fostered. Moreover, as one uses the same critical methods to study the religious literatures of other people, such as the Moslem Quran or the Hindu Upanishads, the walls which separate religions begin to crumble. It becomes increasingly difficult to maintain that our Bible as interpreted by our denomination is the exclusive expression of religious truth and all others are "wrong" if not deliberately sinful. One can no longer label the other religions as evil forces upon which the demons which lie in one's own psyche can be projected. This change of attitude is no small blessing in a world where the arrogant claims of Fundamentalism, be it that of the Ayatollah Khomeini or of the television evangelist, promote divisiveness and hatred in a world where the presence of nuclear weapons could turn petty conflicts into the tragic destruction of the whole human family. I believe that most historico-critical scholars would applaud the move towards inclusivity which is one of the results of their work. This is just one indication that we are not as value-free as we sometimes would like to pretend.

For the Catholic Church and the mainline Protestant churches, the transition from pre-critical to critical has already been made as far as the community of scholars and the church leaders are concerned. Nevertheless, it often happens that the individual, even in these denominations, has grown up with a pre-critical, quasi-fundamentalist attitude towards the Bible. The whole struggle which took place on the ecclesial level is replayed on the individual level when such a person is exposed to critical study of the Bible. The process is often accompanied by intense inner conflict and pain. Nonetheless, the crisis can be an opportunity for personal growth in which the initially negative impact of the critical perspective turns into decidedly positive results. It is helpful to compare this crisis to the change of attitude towards parents which takes place in adolescence. The small child genuinely believes that "my mommy and daddy are the best mommy and daddy in the world"; all their beliefs and values are to be accepted; their directions are to be obeyed and never questioned. We know that it is psychologically normal and healthy for this childish naiveté to go through a crisis, sometimes accompanied by conflict and rebellion, in which the child gains a more objective assessment of the parents and progresses along the path of individuation and independence. If the crisis is passed through successfully, the child will have a different relationship to the parents. There will still be love, respect and the feeling that there is something unique and special about this relationship and these specific human individuals. At the same time, the children will realize that it is meaningless to try to maintain that their parents are "the best mommy and daddy in the world," or to accept all their beliefs and values uncritically. Similarly, most of us began our interest in the Bible at a stage of naiveté in which we regarded our own religious tradition as the only one which was true ("the best"); everything it said was accepted at face value; it was to be respected and obeyed, but never questioned. The individual's introduction to historico-critical scholarship then triggers the crisis in which one has the opportunity to "grow up" in connection with the religious tradition, just as one has had to "grow up" in connection with the parents. It happens quite frequently that it is an introductory Bible course in college that occasions such a crisis. It is one of the privileges of the teacher to serve as guide in this "passage." And it is one of the blessings bestowed by historico-critical scholarship that it has served as the means of our growing up.

So far we have been dealing with results of critical study which at first were experienced negatively but were ultimately positive. We must also speak of contributions which are positive in a more direct sense and which begin to appear after the crisis phase has been passed through. Here I think first of all of the excitement of discovery which I experienced and which I see in many of my students. A whole range of matters which had never made sense to us, some of which we had puzzled over for a long time, suddenly became intelligible. Perhaps we had been disturbed by the presence of duplications and inconsistencies in the book of Genesis. Upon learning that the book is a composite made up of contributions from a number of different sources, the reaction might be, "Aha! Of course. That makes sense." The prophetic books, so confusing if one tries to read them without guidance, searching for logical or thematic continuity, start to become intelligible when one understands the characteristic literary genres employed by the prophets and the historical context in which each passage originated. On a broader scale, the Old Testament as a whole begins to make sense within the context of ancient Near Eastern culture and confirms one's intuition that the Bible could not simply have dropped "out of the blue." For many of us, making such discoveries is utterly fascinating. The more we learn, the more we want to learn, for there seems to be a whole new world of knowledge out there of which we have just a glimpse. It seems that we will never get enough of it. Even if it remains principally on a descriptive and historical plane, this kind of study can be a consuming interest. For some the excitement may last only a short period of time, for others it seems to last much longer, even a whole lifetime in some cases.

In addition to the appeal it has in satisfying our need to understand things on a literary or historical level, historico-critical study of the Bible often makes significant contributions to an individual's search for theological understanding. When a person first realizes that what critical scholarship says about the original meaning of a biblical text may be completely different from what one was taught previously, this discovery might be disturbing. What very frequently happens, however, is that this original meaning ends up looking more attractive to the student than the view he or she was previously taught. For example, the Old Testament does not contain the notion of "soul" which traditional Christian theology learned from Greek philosophers and so the whole venture of ancient Israel has absolutely nothing to do with "saving your soul" or going to heaven after you die. To many contemporary persons, the Old Testament idea that God's blessings relate to the whole person in this life will make more sense than what they were taught in Sunday School. Another example is provided by the conclusion reached by many critical scholars that the revelation of God in the Old Testament is the self-communication of a person who is manifested in the concrete events experienced in the life of the community and the individual rather than in abstract propositional doctrines. Many students will be more comfortable with such a view than with the scholasticism of so much traditional theology. Finally, we can mention that the original teachings of the early church or of Jesus himself, as reconstructed by historico-critical scholarship, are often more appealing than what one learned from the teaching or practice of the churches.

Critical scholarship, then, makes a positive contribution by suggesting theological alternatives. Those who embrace and appropriate these alternatives experience the process as one of growth, moving in a direction of progress in their own theological understanding. Even abstracting from the specific content of the new ideas which develop, I personally agree that it is a gain when persons have more alternatives to choose from and feel free to make responsible choices. There is, of course, a possible danger in that one simply shifts from accepting the authority of a church to the acceptance of critical scholarship as "the authority" which determines what we should think about religious issues. It cannot be denied that many people seem to bestow this mantle of authority on scholarship and that there are unfortunately many scholars who are only too glad to tell people what they should believe on the basis of what is allegedly proved by scientific study. However, the continued pursuit of critical study, if it is carried on with true openness and honesty, itself militates against such neo-authoritarianism. For one becomes aware of the great variety of conclusions reached by critical scholars and the broad range of issues concerning which we really do not know the answers. For example, though critical scholars agree that the Pentateuch is a composite work, there is no agreement as to how many sources entered into its composition, where those sources came from, or how they are to be dated. It is especially on theological matters that, even on the descriptive level, scholars cannot reach agreement. What is the meaning of Job or Ecclesiastes? What did Isaiah, the son of Amoz, believe concerning the Davidic kingship and the divine protection of Jerusalem? How was the function of animal sacrifice understood in ancient Israelite religion? Which of the sayings attributed to Jesus in the New Testament are "authentic" and what did they originally mean? There is no consensus on these issues and there probably never will be. And that brings us to a consideration of the limitations of the historico-critical method.

3. The Limitations of the Historico-Critical Method

The question of the limitations of the historico-critical method is quite a controversial topic. On the one side there are very conservative or Fundamentalist theologians who believe that the whole historico-critical venture was misguided, even pernicious, from the start. They are always delighted to have anyone point out its limitations. On the other side there are practitioners of the historico-critical approach who have been under sometimes vicious attack from the right wing. These persons tend to get nervous about the questioning of the critical approach because they fear it just gives more ammunition to their reactionary opponents. The preceding section of this Appendix should make it clear that in this book we are taking a favorable attitude towards the critical approach, but at the same time we want to move beyond it in order to attain some goals which the historico-critical method, strictly speaking, cannot reach on its own.

The diversity of opinions about the adequacy of historico-critical study found in discussions among scholars and theologians is also reflected among students. It often happens that students who do not have any particularly conservative axe to grind, and who may even have been enthusiastic about critical study for some period of time, begin to express reservations. They may complain that the method is too pre-occupied with irrelevant historical facts; that there is endless dissecting and analyzing of minute details which have no connection with any kind of significant meaning; that it is too intellectual and academic, it is dead and boring, it has no connection with anything real in people's lives. When such issues are raised in class, it is frequently some of the other students who will counter these criticisms, saying something like, "Oh no! This is fascinating. When you get into this you start understanding how the ancient Israelites thought and believed and I find it connects in all kinds of ways with things that are important in my life." I must confess that I do not know what accounts for the difference between these two groups of students nor whether the ones who are currently enthusiastic will eventually become disillusioned too. But it is not necessary to answer these questions. It is a fact which all teachers encounter that at least a significant number of students are dissatisfied with what historico-critical study can give them. Since there is a clear need for something more, then it is important for us to investigate ways of reaching that "more."

Perhaps the most incisive critique of the historico-critical method published in recent years is a small book entitled *The Bible in Human Transformation* (Philadelphia: Fortress Press, 1973) by Walter Wink. The book opens dramatically with the declaration that, "Historical biblical criticism is bankrupt." Wink does not mean by this that it is worthless and should be abandoned, but that it needs to be put under new management if it is ever to achieve its goal, which he formulates as follows: "so to interpret the Scriptures that the past becomes alive and illumines our present with new possibilities for personal and social transformation."

Wink argues that when the critical method deliberately

practices "detached neutrality" it cuts itself off from dealing with precisely those issues (such as faith and conversion) which were most important to the biblical authors themselves. Such a method, then, would be intrinsically inadequate for fully understanding the biblical literature. As a matter of fact, however, there is no such thing as a completely neutral, detached, objective method. The historico-critical approach does have a commitment to a certain way of understanding reality and even to a specific value system. Wink claims that it is naive, if not outright dishonest, to fail to recognize and acknowledge the bias inherent in the methodology. Furthermore, the method as it is now practiced, serves the self-interest of the academic guild of scholars and leads to ever greater separation between the results of this study and the real-life concerns of human beings.

These issues, succinctly delineated by Wink, have been the center of intense discussion within a relatively small circle of scholars concerned with "hermeneutical" questions. Unfortunately, the scholarly community as a whole has tended to ignore the problems. In any case, it is not necessary for our purposes to become involved in the details of philosophical and methodological controversy. Instead, I would like to make use of a paradigm which Wink has adapted from the writings of Paul Ricoeur to sum up the way things stand at present and point to the direction in which we must move.

The paradigm presented by Wink delineates three stages in a dialectical process which can be outlined as follows:

1. FUSION   (First Naiveté)

2. DISTANCE   (Historico-Critical Process)

3. COMMUNION   (Second Naiveté)

The stage of fusion or first naiveté is the one where most of us began our relationship with the Bible. We identified with it as completely as a child identifies with its parents. That blissful state is disturbed by the negative impact of critical study in which we create distance between ourselves and the Bible. The Bible becomes an object-out-there which we manipulate and control in order to wrest its secrets. We feel free to dominate the text, tearing it apart, questioning it, attaining mastery over it. This moment of distancing, at which the historico-critical method excels, appears to be just as necessary and unavoidable as the adolescent crisis through which a child must reach a new relationship with the parents. The problem, says Wink, is that the historico-critical method has become stuck at this second stage. Indeed, as the critical method is usually understood, we are forced to conclude that on its own it is incapable of going any further. Yet a meaningful relationship with the Bible requires that we pass beyond the distancing stage to a position of communion which can be called the second naiveté. This second naiveté differs from the innocence of the first stage, for once having gone through the critical experience we have been profoundly and permanently changed. Nonetheless we must seek for ways in which we can make ourselves open to the transformative power of the text. That requires that we pause from working on the text in order to allow it to work on us. In my own interpretation of Wink's paradigm it is this attitude of openness and of surrender, allowing the text to transform us, that justifies the label "second naiveté."

The challenge which faces the discipline of biblical studies today is to find ways of reaching this position of a second naiveté. I do not mean to imply that this is something which has never been done before. For I suspect that there may be many teachers who have employed the critical method and yet in their teaching have pushed on to that "something more" which is necessary for a full personal appropriation of the material. Perhaps it is their unusually high degree of awareness of their own inner process that has instinctively moved such teachers towards that stage of communion which goes with the second naiveté. While their contribution is not to be overlooked, it must be admitted that they constitute an exception to the rule. One need only listen to papers presented at the meetings of scholars such as at the Society of Biblical Literature, or skim the textbooks used in college courses to be convinced that the profession as a whole is stuck at the second stage: Distance!

Where, then, do we go from here? The only possibility, it seems to me, is that those of us who recognize the need which exists must become willing to experiment and to share with others the results of our experimentation. This is exactly what I have attempted to do in the four principal chapters of *Life Journey and the Old Testament.* It is now up to the reader to decide whether the techniques which I am proposing effectively provide access to the transformative power of the Bible for people's lives, fostering their growth, and furthering them in their life journeys.

NOTE

1. The discrepancy between the traditional understanding of "messianic" prophecies and the conclusions reached by historical criticism creates a significant theological problem. My proposal for solving this problem is presented in "Understanding the Old Testament Prophecies," *The Bible Today* 23 (1985) 51–59.

The visualizations/meditations described in chapters 2, 3 and 4 are available on cassette tape.

For information, contact:

LIFE JOURNEYS
335 Spirea Drive
Dayton, Ohio 45419
(513) 297-0793